THE LAST MILE

THE LAST MILE

India's Experiments with Rural Finance

R.N. Dash

Foreword by

Dr. Y.V. Reddy

Former Governor, Reserve Bank of India

Konark Publishers Pvt Ltd
New Delhi • Seattle

Konark Publishers Pvt Ltd
206, First Floor,
Peacock Lane, Shahpur Jat,
New Delhi - 110 049
Phone: +91-11-41055065
Mob: +91 93552 93900, +91 93552 94900
e-mail: india@konarkpublishers.com
website: www.konarkpublishers.com

Konark Publishers International
8615, 13th Ave SW,
Seattle, WA 98106
Phone: (415) 409-9988
e-mail: us@konarkpublishers.com

Cataloging in Publication Data—DK
Courtesy: D.K. Agencies (P) Ltd. <docinfo@dkagencies.com>

Dash, R. N. (Ramanath), author.
The last mile : India's experiments with rural finance / R.N. Dash; foreword by Dr. Y.V. Reddy (Former Governor, Reserve Bank of India).
pages cm
Includes bibliographical references and index
ISBN 9789322008710

1. Rural credit—India. 2. Microfinance—India. 3. Banks and banking—India. 4. Rural development—Government policy—India. I. Title.

HG2051.I4D37 2019 DDC 332.710954 23

Edited by Seema Kumar
Jacket Design by Dushyant Parasher
Typeset by The Laser Printers, New Delhi
Printed and bound in India by Thomson Press India Ltd.

Dedicated to my wife Urmila, who has been a constant source of strength, and but for whose help and support it would not have been possible to complete this book.

Contents

Foreword

INDIA, in particular the Reserve Bank of India (RBI), has a long tradition of public policy dealing with rural credit. At the time of its inception in 1935, an important task for the RBI in the broad area of credit was promotion of agricultural credit. The main focus was to assist the provincial governments in the consolidation and expansion of cooperative credit institutions. This included providing financial accommodation to cooperative banks. Subsequently, the RBI was closely involved in the formulation of the post-war plans concerning rural credit. The All India Rural Credit Survey of 1951-52 brought to the fore the enormity of problems relating to rural credit. One of the fallouts was the establishment of the State Bank of India through nationalisation in 1955 to extend banking facilities 'in the rural and semi-urban areas'.

The exclusive focus on promoting the flow of agricultural credit through cooperatives changed in 1966 when the concept of social control over commercial banks was introduced. From the mid-1960s, the role of the RBI became more varied and several agencies such as Agricultural Refinancing Corporation came into existence. With the nationalisation of major banks in 1969, the expansion of branches in rural areas became a priority. The policies of rural credits were targeted towards vulnerable sections, and expansion of credit was the goal. Simultaneously, an integrated and area-based approach at different levels, namely village, block, district and state was taken up. Institutional arrangements were devised for collaboration with the state governments. Two major innovations in the 1970s and 1980s are the setting up of Regional Rural Banks in 1975 and National Bank for Agriculture and Rural Development (NABARD) in 1982. Cross-subsidisation was also accepted as a conscious policy. However, in the process, the regulatory guidelines and directives compromised the prudential aspects of banking. The whole process was considered a development-cum-egalitarian approach, often described as social banking and mass banking with target orientation. Unfortunately, the viability of such activities financed by credit was not given attention. This period initiated the area of poor recoveries and increasing non-performing assets.

The intellectual orientation was that credit for productive activities is good; for agriculture, it is essential; for the vulnerable, it is deserving. But, where does that money come from? From the depositors, who by no means are the rich; from the capital of bank, especially public sector banks and from the RBI.

Is money created by the RBI (for refinancing) a 'free good'? Apparently, it is, but in reality, not. If countries could move out of poverty by printing money, no country would be poor. Very few asked such questions till the time the reforms were initiated.

The Narasimham Committee on the Financial System, 1991, commented, 'The emphasis was on providing credit and there was no equal emphasis on recovery of credit.' Though this was said in 1991, the position broadly remains the same now as far as rural credit is concerned.

There are several concerns in relation to rural credit which are generally expressed in terms of inadequacy, constraints on timely availability, high cost, neglect of small and marginal farmers, low credit-deposit ratios in several states and continued presence of informal markets. It is held that while the commercial banks are more focused on improving efficiency and profitability, they have tended to give comparatively less priority to rural credit. Regional Rural Banks (RRBs) and cooperatives appear to face serious problems of governance as well as operational efficiency. It is argued that most part of the cooperative credit structure is multi-layered, under-capitalised, over-staffed and under-skilled, often with mounting non-performing assets and in a few cases, resulting in erosion of public deposits as well. Many RRBs also appear to share most of these problems, though there are some vibrant and viable institutions in this category. These problems relating to rural credit have been well documented, and several policy approaches were made to remedy the situation. However, there is some element of dissatisfaction that the overall situation with regard to rural credit is not improving to the desired level in spite of such a series of actions.

It is not as though there were no policy initiatives and most of them appear to be, as R. N. Dash, the author of this book, describes India's experiments with rural finance. The book captures what may be described as a new way of approaching the new initiatives as a work in progress. We now talk not merely of rural credit but of financial services. The book considers policy making in the context of supply-push and demand-pull. In doing so, technology is both an opportunity and a challenge.

The experiments, described in the book, cover institutions and instruments to expand the supply side of credit to rural areas. These include recourse to the banking correspondent model, encouraging micro finance institutions, involving non-banking finance companies and, more recently, establishment of small banks. Institutional innovations like self-help groups and local area banks were also attempted. The RBI ceased to create money for agriculture but decided to do so for the government only. The government could correspondingly get enhanced access to the resources from the RBI for its use.

In recent years, there was a shift from credit to finance, as the sub-title of the book says, 'India started experimenting with rural finance'. Providing access to financial services including, in particular, savings account and credit for consumption smoothening, became part of policy instruments. True mass banking was enabled by developments in technology. This resulted in huge savings in the cost of delivery and provision of financial services in general.

What is the current status? The overall growth in the agricultural credit is slow; the timely availability of credit has worsened; and the viability of agricultural operations is under stress and the risk element in commercial agriculture is increasing.

Agriculture has become more of a gamble than before due to policy-enabled risks such as unreliable quality of seeds, fertilisers, power, and water. The prices for farmers' products are subject to policy changes either in the interest of the consumer or external sector balance. The difference in the rate of growth of rural and urban areas, in particular agricultural and non-agricultural areas, is becoming glaring.

This has led to two sets of reactions, namely clamour for loan waivers and farmer suicides.

In brief, our record of performance with regard to rural credit has been more of innovations and attempts and less of achievement in terms of outcomes.

We have invested, experimented, innovated and reformed credit and more recently rural credit. We have genuine doubts about what we have achieved. Perhaps, it is time we asked new questions.

First, how much of the rural finance issue is a reflection of the financial sector, including banking as a whole, and how much is the issue unique to rural areas or agriculture?

Second, is credit culture in rural areas different from others? Is loan waiver not similar to restructuring and write-off?

Third, how much is the overall all-in-cost of credit in agriculture, that is, including transaction costs, documentation and repeated visits, etc., as a percentage of the loan?

Fourth, how much of agriculture is commercially viable?

Fifth, what types of risks are covered by crop insurance? Is it mostly insurance of loans extended?

Is it true that the problems and solutions for rural finance go beyond finance and agriculture?

How about the future? The approach for the future may have to be in terms of making agriculture more productive, more commercially viable and less vulnerable to risks and shocks. This does not mean that we should give up our attempts to improve the capabilities of the financial sector to serve rural areas and agriculture. In fact, the financial sector may not be the lead sector for agricultural growth.

We must be aware that over the medium to long term, the share of agriculture in the GDP will have to come down. The number of people depending on agriculture will have to come down drastically, and the population residing in rural areas will also have to come down correspondingly.

The stark choice is dividing our limited resources between inevitable shrinking of rural economies in particular agriculture, and inevitably expanding urban and manufacturing services.

There exists considerable literature on the subject and the question is why another one on rural finance? This book is a primer par excellence on rural credit. It is a valuable addition to the literature on the state of rural finance and the way forward. It is commendable for the unique approach it takes to the problem, namely an integrated view of technology, policy and financial service.

I congratulate the author for producing an informative and authentic work on a contentious subject.

Dr Y. V. Reddy
Former Governor, Reserve Bank of India

May 2, 2018

B. YERRAM RAJU, M.A., Ph.D.
Advisor
Telangana Industrial Health Clinic Ltd.
Parisrama Bhavanam, Basheerbagh,
HYDERABAD-500 004.

2-19-57/B, Kalyanapuri,
Uppal, Hyderabad - 500 039
Phone : [R]+91-40-27201592
[M]+91-98852 96111
yerramr@gmail. com
erram@tihcl.org
www.tihcl.telangana.gov.in

The Last Mile

India's Experiments with Rural Finance

Author: R.N. Dash

The Author, with a reputation as a responsible regulator, has displayed his passion in a very lucid style on a very intricate subject—'Rural Finance' in India. The rural finance sphere has more enemies than friends—right from weather to wealth. Institutional interventions in this vast democracy have always been found inadequate. Innovations have always been welcomed but with suspicion.

The book has six chapters with the meat in Chapter 3: The Demand Factor—Facilitating First Mile Walk. Demand has always exceeded supply and it is unstructured. Clientele is highly heterogeneous and with esoteric demands. Supply side issues have been dealt with exhaustively. With a big gap between supply and demand in the rural finance space still posing enormous challenges highlighted in the book, the author's suggestions are worth the attention of policy makers and regulators.

This book fills the gap in literature on rural finance and provides scope for further research. Researchers, academicians, practitioners of rural banking and policy makers will immensely benefit by reading the book. The author deserves rich compliments for his lucid and facile narration of a subject writ with complexities.

10th May 2018

B. Yerram Raju

Preface

WITH an increase in population and increasing exposure to the world outside, there has been a paradigm shift in the lifestyle and perception of the people in rural areas. Agriculture still continues to be the most important occupation but other activities in the non-farm sector and the services segment have caught up with it. The aspirations and the world view of people have changed. A continuous provision of money is required not only for maintaining the development process, but also for meeting the increasing expectations and aspirations of the youth.

The rural sector has been increasingly viewed as a vast market waiting to be tapped. Companies have focused their attention on this segment as it has provided ample opportunities outside the overcrowded urban market. The peculiarities of demand in the rural economy have been studied to design appropriate products and services for the rural market so as to take advantage of the 'fortune at the bottom of the pyramid'. The role of finance has become extremely important in this scenario. Historically, banks were brought in to supplement the efforts of the government in meeting the financial needs of an expanding economy and in ensuring integrated rural development; several other entities have also seen the opportunities and have become active players in this market. The whole system has become highly complex, and the developments highly fascinating.

My stint in the Reserve Bank of India (RBI), especially in the erstwhile Rural Planning and Credit Department, has given me ample opportunity to follow these developments closely. I have had the benefit of working in the areas of policy making, teaching and practising rural finance and financial inclusion. My association with several important committees, set up by the RBI and the Government of India, also gave me an insight into the issues and challenges facing the rural sector as well as an understanding of how the people themselves viewed the situation. This was amply helped by the outreach visits conducted by the RBI during its Platinum Jubilee year and later, which provided me an opportunity to directly interact with the people and to understand their viewpoint.

One thing that became clear was that the country has been continuously experimenting since the beginning of the previous century to provide adequate finance to meet the requirements of the rural sector. Institutions have been set up, policies have been put in place, programmes have been designed and implemented; yet we cannot confidently say that we have been able to achieve our goal of providing financial services to all as per their needs. The external world has changed fast, throwing up new challenges. Technology has permeated the financial sector in a truly unprecedented manner. All this has called for more experimentation in design and delivery of rural financial services. And, the process of experimentation continues.

In the good old days, credit was at the centre of financial services delivery in the rural sector. The policy mainly focused on the availability of credit for agriculture and related areas. Replacement of the moneylender or the informal source of finance by formal financial institutions dominated the thought process. With time, provision of other financial services, such as savings or thrift, and insurance, has also assumed importance, as the emphasis has moved to financial inclusion. The demand side of the process has emerged as a major issue and financial education for the common person has assumed urgency.

The book captures this evolving process and the changing priorities associated with it. It is an attempt to paint a comprehensive picture of rural finance from the policy and practice viewpoint. In the process of covering all the developments that have occurred over time, certain areas have not been dealt with in detail. There are well written books, which focus on separate activities and fields. These will be excellent supplements to this book. My endeavour has been to present an overview, a snapshot, in very simple terms, which would be useful both to the practitioners and policy makers as well as the general readers interested in this lively field of rural finance in India.

Acknowledgements

THIS book is the result not only of my fairly long association with and study of the domain of rural finance but also my interaction with several people, comprising practitioners and experts in this field. In writing the book, I have also drawn upon existing literature in the form of books, articles in journals, newspapers and websites. I have made an attempt to include a list of the reference material at the end. I am indebted to all the experts, writers and commentators for enriching my knowledge and shaping my views on the interesting, but at the same time complicated, subject of rural finance and development.

Any endeavour of this kind needs the blessings of great men who have shaped our views over a period of time. I am grateful to Dr Y.V. Reddy, former Governor, Reserve Bank of India and an acknowledged authority in the field of banking and finance, for patiently going through the manuscript, offering guidance and suggestions at several places and for taking the pains to write the Foreword which provides a glimpse into the evolving world of rural finance in India and the role of the Central Bank. I am also grateful to Dr P. Kotaiah, former Chairman, National Bank for Agriculture and Rural Development (NABARD), who not only welcomed the writing of the book but also went through the manuscript in great detail and offered valuable suggestions, based upon his vast experience and insight. I have greatly benefitted from the vast experience and knowledge of Dr B. Yerram Raju, eminent economist, author and an acknowledged expert in the field of rural finance, who has also gone through the manuscript minutely and offered valuable suggestions to improve the coverage and quality of the presentation. I am grateful to him for his encouragement and support for publishing this book.

My friends and former colleagues at the Reserve Bank of India, Manas Ranjan Mohanty, Chief General Manager, an expert in this field, Dr Singala Subbaiah, General Manager, who was heading the Financial Inclusion and Development Department at RBI, Hyderabad, and Suvendu Pati, General Manager, RBI, Hyderabad, have patiently gone through the first draft and offered valuable suggestions. Their encouragement has, in fact, helped me in further improving the write-up in several areas.

My son, Rahul Dash, an excellent writer, was the first to offer his comments when the book was conceived some time back. Since then he has been tracking the developments and encouraging me to complete the project in time. I am thankful to him for all this. The main force behind writing this book is none other than my wife, Urmila Dash, who has solidly stood by me through all the vicissitudes and offered her unstinting support and encouragement. But for her, the book would perhaps have not seen the light of the day. I am grateful to her for everything that she has done.

For a first-time writer, publishing a book is often a big challenge. I am fortunate to have been introduced to K.P.R. Nair, Managing Director, Konark Publishers Pvt Ltd, who, apart from encouraging me went ahead and published the book. I am thankful to him and his excellent team at Konark Publishers Pvt Ltd for all the support and guidance. It has been a great experience working with the team.

Last, but not the least, I have interacted with several people in the villages which I visited from time to time, both in my official capacity and otherwise. I also interacted with various stakeholders on several occasions, during meetings, study visits and during my association with committees in the past. It will be difficult to name all of them but I am thankful to all for their contribution, which helped me in completing this book.

1

Financial Services in Rural India – Work in Progress

THE scorching sun could not stop Venkata Reddy, a small farmer in Mehboobnagar district of Telangana State, from going out to his field. He was used to this. Last year, he had harvested a normal crop of rice in the same field. The harvest was good for all the villagers, so much so that the price at harvest time had gone to an all-time low. He had somehow managed to sell a part of the produce to the local trader and paid interest on the loan he had taken from the village moneylender. The loan he had taken from a local bank, however, remained unpaid. Like many others in the village, he had expected this year to be somewhat better. He had planned to repay the entire loan and perhaps take another to make some improvement on the only piece of land he owned. There were other expenses also to be taken care of. The weather god, however, played a very cruel game and whatever cloud was seen in the sky in the beginning of June vanished soon. It had become another long wait for heaven's mercy but nothing was coming. Paddy had been sown but the plants could not survive the dry weather. This was not the first time the rains had played truant. He had, in fact, seen such situations many times before – sometimes drought, sometimes heavy rains. The only problem was the unexpectedness of it all. It was just not possible to plan or calculate anything. Something was going terribly wrong somewhere. Will the loan waiver being promised by some politicians help, at least temporarily? How far will the subsidised inputs, assured by the government, meet the requirements of the next sowing season? Could he rely on the quality of seed available in the market? What if next year also turned out to be as bad or even worse? He took a long look at the parched earth and sighed.

Venkata Reddy is not alone. Millions like Reddy face a similar situation every year in some place, in some corner of the country. In fact, the story is familiar to all of us having some experience of the rural and agricultural sector in our country. Agriculture in this country has many serious issues. Financial matters constitute just one of them. But finance has the potential to impact several other areas. Getting a loan on time and on easy terms, being able to utilise it and also repay it in time, getting some insurance cover for unexpected loss arising out of bad weather, bad inputs, bad price, bad policy, or just bad luck, are all issues that our farmers have been grappling with for decades. They have learnt to live with all these and to protect themselves in their own way to some extent from the multiple risks. The system has, however, not helped them much. Somehow, this sector has got largely bypassed by the progress shown by the country on many other fronts. In many parts of the country, people like Venkata Reddy are still waiting for some safe, reliable, predictable and effective way of accessing finance to carry out their activities, which many consider inherently risky, but which everyone knows are essential for our survival. What has gone wrong? And, can there be a lasting solution to these problems?

Far from Reddy's field, in a remote village in the coastal district of East Godavari in Andhra Pradesh, some villagers have lined up before a fair price shop. They have their Aadhaar cards in hand. Some of them carry the smart cards issued by a Business Correspondent. The Business Correspondent at the fair price shop checks their fingerprints on a hand held Micro ATM, keys in some numbers and waits patiently for a response. This is the Aadhaar Enabled Payment System (AEPS) through which direct cash transfers are made to the bank accounts of the beneficiaries of some schemes by the government, post which they can withdraw cash with the help of the POS machines (also called Micro ATMs)[1]. Apart from making the process more transparent, this is also a case where technology has helped the mainstream players. Everyone in the country knew the electronic age had arrived, but a decade ago, not many could think that payment systems would develop in a way so as to enable the villagers in remote areas access financial services in the manner just described. Is this then the ultimate stage of a series of experiments for providing financial services in a cost-effective manner to those who do not have access to banks at the moment for a variety of reasons?

Move on to Devarapalli, a small non-descript village in the tribal belt of the same district. Till not long ago, the village did not even have an all-weather road. Agriculture being the major occupation of the people, many of them needed financial assistance to carry out their farm activities year after year, and even for consumption smoothing. The village had potential to grow rubber. Those in the village, who were somewhat better off, used to travel to a bank branch about five miles away and get loans. For others, banking seemed to be a distant idea, not connected with their daily lives. As it happens, life just dragged on in this sleepy village, not much different from many others all over the country. It appeared as though time just stood still, until one day when the village suddenly witnessed a flurry of activity. Some well-dressed persons in cars arrived in the village, and the villagers were called to a meeting at the primary school ground. There some officials explained to them the benefits of dealing with banks, how to save money and why bank loans needed to be repaid in time. Promises were made by the speakers to bring banking to the village itself. This was a financial literacy drive by some banks operating in the district. People gathered there mostly out of curiosity. They listened and went back home. And then slowly, the change happened. Today, after a few years, Devarapalli is known as a model village. There is a satellite office of a bank, which operates twice a week in the village. The road has improved and so has education and training. Taking note of the developments, the Rubber Board arranged a special training programme for the villagers on rubber processing. There is a Business Correspondent of a bank who travels to the village regularly and provides deposit and withdrawal facilities, the basic cash transactions. Life has, to some extent, changed for the villagers of Devarapalli; but what about other such villages dotting the map of our country?

Srinivas Murthy is a young man hailing from another village in remote Kurnool district, located near the famous Nandi Temple of Nandyal. A school dropout, he is looking for odd jobs to make a living and help his family. Like in Devarapalli, banks had also conducted an awareness camp in his village a couple of years ago around the same time. But unlike the village in East Godavari, no such development has taken place in this village, where people still wait for the promises to be fulfilled and some development to take place. Murthy says he was given to understand that this would ultimately lead to economic prosperity as banks would come, listen to them and give loans. The expectations aroused by the event have subsequently not materialised. As it is, development is a complex phenomenon, having several stakeholders, both at the causation and outcome levels. The vicious circle of 'poverty-low income-low savings-low assets-poverty' has to be broken at some point to let a person rise above that level and aspire for a decent life. There have been several attempts in the past to bring about this change. So how to make financial services provide the trigger for this? Everybody in the village he spoke to seemed pessimistic and callous. Srinivas Murthy is fast losing hope.

The story is not unique to these two states. Similar situations exist in all the states in the country. In today's world, we take so many things for granted, including financial services. All of us need financial services as we deal with goods and services and with money. Only our needs are different and needs also change with time and place. The story is the same in the case of the villagers. They need a safe place to deposit their money, some loan on favourable and simple terms in time of need, a secure way of remitting and receiving money and some reliable insurance facilities to take care of unforeseen events. Requirements as usual will vary depending on occupations and cash flow and maybe the family composition and the time of the year. In the good old days, when there were no banks and things were not so monetised, people used to get the services they wanted from an informal sector or by way of a barter system. It used to be so common that not many even noticed it. While time-tested informal modes are still available, the costs involved and risks associated with these are generally very high. Hence institutional alternatives are imperative. Rural credit policy in this country has evolved in such a manner that the focus has always been on elimination of this so-called informal sector. Some mechanisms have evolved with time, while some others have been created through conscious intervention. Each mechanism, however, proves successful in a certain specific context. And an ever-changing ground level situation changes the context and calls for continuous, newer experiments.

Experiments have been happening on both the supply and demand sides of financial services as they are related to the lives and needs of the people in rural areas. The scope to experiment in the financial domain is, however, much less on the demand side. Several people we are talking about have actually never undertaken a financial transaction at any bank or financial institution, and for them the first mile walk into the financial system is itself a big achievement. That leaves us with the reality that most of the experiments happen in the domain of the suppliers of financial services and products, either at their own initiative or under regulatory policy intervention.

India is predominantly a rural economy, with 68.8 per cent of its population and 72.4 per cent of the workforce living in rural areas (as per the 2011 Census). Rural economy contributes 46 per cent of the national income. Population projections indicate that India will continue to be predominantly rural till 2050, after which the urban population is expected to overtake the rural population[2]. Thus the growth and development of the rural economy is a key determinant of the growth and development of the country. The demand for financial services is closely associated with the developments in real economy and the nature of economic activities undertaken by the people. It is also influenced by their lifestyle, education and literacy level, including the level of financial literacy and awareness about financial products and markets. Rural economy in India is also predominantly agriculture-based. Agriculture has vital supply-and-demand links with the other industries. Agriculture constitutes the backbone of rural India, even as small enterprises and non-farm sector activities including the service sector enterprises are showing an increasing share in the rural GDP. Therefore, the demand for financial services, to a great extent, gets shaped by the contours of agriculture and related activities. The profile of agriculture in this country is such that it covers a wide spectrum, starting from the landless and tenant farmers to marginal and small farmers and then to medium and large farmers. Financial requirements are linked to the part of the spectrum we are talking about. At the lower end of the spectrum, we have the financially excluded groups for whom financial access itself is a problem and separate approaches and strategies are required, not only to ensure availability of services and products but also to stimulate demand for the same. Most of the financial inclusion activities we see today are directed at this segment of the population.

The effectiveness of all these measures, however, varies with the efforts made to turn sustenance agriculture into a sustainable proposition and with the linkages that can be established between the real sector and the financial sector at the base level. Finance cannot stand on its own; it needs support from the real sector. To be truly successful, financial inclusion must go hand-in-hand with overall economic inclusion. As we conduct financial literacy and inclusion campaigns in villages and elsewhere, we must ensure that economic activities also pick up, depending on the local resources available and through suitable up-skilling of the people, so that money actually flows into and out of bank accounts. The money in the account can be put either by the person himself, if he has some cash flow, or by the bank, through a loan or overdraft scheme, or at least by the government, under one of the many schemes aimed at providing financial assistance to the people. Without any such supporting mechanism, left to the person, there won't be any transaction in these accounts and the laudable goal of financial inclusion will remain on paper. If we are serious about development, banks and the government must sit together, along with other local agencies, and discuss across the table about ways to make these things happen. To be fair, we do have mechanisms and systems in place for all these but over a period of time, these have become routine and compliance-oriented.

Development of the rural sector has always been a major focus of our national policy and so far as funding is concerned, much of the initiative has centred around provision of timely and adequate credit in rural areas. In essence, financial inclusion (although the phrase came to currency in the last decade of the previous century) has been equated with giving a loan. As people lacked resources, providing them a loan for some purpose was considered the most important way to address poverty and improve their standard of living. Providing a loan itself has passed through different stages. Apart from moneylenders and other such elements, which constituted the informal system, the government was in the past, to a limited extent, providing credit to farmers directly in the form of Taccavi loans[3]. Even as cooperative societies came up and were supported by the government since the first decade of the last century, they had made limited headway on account of low penetration and limited numbers. Even there, the needs of small and marginal farmers generally got overlooked in favour of big farmers. It was not surprising, therefore, that in 1950-51, non-institutional agents accounted for as much as 92.8 per cent share in rural credit, while institutional sources (the government, co-operative societies and commercial banks) accounted for a mere 7.2 per cent[4].

After Independence and the launch of the era of planned process of development in India, a number of agricultural and rural development programmes were drawn up and implemented both by the Central and state governments. Many of these programmes required credit linkage and increasingly, the banking system was looked upon as a partner in this development process initiated by the government. The existing banking structure was not suitable for this work and had to be tweaked or transformed to conform to the policy requirements. Nationalisation of the Imperial Bank of India (to State Bank of India) was done in the 1950s. Nationalisation of major commercial banks followed in 1969 and in 1980. New institutions such as Regional Rural Banks (RRBs) and NABARD were created to take care of the emerging developmental needs. Over a period of time, a multi-agency approach to rural credit emerged, in which cooperative banks, commercial banks and RRBs shared the responsibility of providing credit for the rural and agricultural sector, each having its share of strengths and weaknesses.

This focus on credit provision by banks and financial institutions remained and lending to the priority sector, comprising agriculture, small industries, small business and similar activities, became an important yardstick for measuring the performance of banks immediately after nationalisation. This exclusive emphasis on lending and the consequent clamour to achieve the targets at any cost were to a large extent responsible for the decline in the health of the cooperative banks earlier, as they never really bothered about the source of funds, which came through the multi-level institutional structure. The exclusive focus on credit also influenced the financial discipline in commercial banks in those days and the way RRBs performed till the mid-1990s. In a sense, this lack of concern for the source of funds and lack of emphasis on where the money comes from, as long as it is available for spending, has become a part of our systemic thinking. That is probably why not many really bother when politicians make public announcements of nebulous schemes requiring huge funds that are nowhere to be seen, make promises to write off bank loans or exhort borrowers not to repay, and when banks on their own write off huge sums of debt owed by the industries, trade and agriculture. This thinking is also largely responsible for the increasing involvement of banks in financing a large number of government-sponsored programmes, knowing pretty well that much of these loans are going to be mis-utilised and hence not repaid by the borrowers. An associated fact is the tolerance of loan default in the system. Although everybody knows that banks are but custodians of public money and must get the loans back in time with interest, yet many actually sympathise with a loan defaulter, unless, of course, he is a high-profile wilful defaulter.

It has taken quite some time to explicitly recognise as a matter of public policy that the people staying in rural areas also need financial services other than loans and to realise that such financial services could perhaps be delivered in a sustainable and cost-effective manner. In neighbouring Bangladesh, the microcredit revolution in the early 1970s showed the way to bank with the poor, and Microfinance Institutions (MFIs) proved that lending to the poor need not always be poor lending. The Self Help Group (SHG) model developed in India and the subsequent linkage of SHGs with banks opened up a way to channelise bank finance to the poor in a sustainable manner. Although MFIs have subsequently run into trouble for certain reasons, which we shall see later, the basic fact remains that they have empirically proved that an institutional mechanism can be evolved to provide small doses of finance to the poor depending on their needs and exigencies, without sacrificing the institution's survival and that a visit to the moneylender is not a fait accompli for the villagers.

From microfinance to financial inclusion was only a logical journey. Microfinance in India emphasised not only loans but also savings (thrift) and in many cases, insurance and remittance of funds. Several experiments were seen taking place in different parts of the globe regarding designing of microfinancial products and services for the poor, including in India. The concept of financial inclusion provided a framework for the provision of a basket of services to the people, who for various reasons remained excluded from the formal financial system. The SHG-bank linkage in India, pioneered by the National Bank for Agriculture and Rural Development (NABARD), proceeded on the belief that saving was more important for the poor than loans. The financial inclusion experiment also started with making savings facilities available to people to put their hard earned money safely[5]. In fact, one hears anecdotes about how in some villages, poor labourers used to hide currency notes stuffed in bamboo hollows tugged in the roof of thatched houses. This proves our hypothesis that if people need some service, they will find some way of getting it somewhere, maybe that will be risky and costly but services will be available to them anyway. This also goes to prove the continued existence of the so-called informal sector of finance in our villages and towns.

The move for financial inclusion in India started in 2005[6]. The banking system, which was at the heart of this massive exercise, accepted this mandate, although with an initial reluctance. The scenario considerably changed when in 2014, the Government of India announced and put its weight behind a comprehensive financial inclusion programme named Pradhan Mantri Jan Dhan Yojana (PMJDY). This programme carried forward the financial inclusion agenda, which till then was moving in fits and starts and had the force to bring the entire banking system to focus on opening basic accounts for the excluded population in record time. Later, it also led to other financial services, such as insurance and pension services aimed at this target group, which could be linked to these accounts and also paved the way for the Government's ambitious programme of channelising payments to beneficiaries of several schemes through bank accounts. In fact, the latter objective was a major driving force for the Government to go in for large-scale opening of bank accounts so that not only would they save on administrative cost but would also plug the leakages associated with the distribution system and handling of physical cash.

Financial services to the rural sector, especially to the poor, in our country have seen a series of experiments over the past, and the experimentation still continues. Institutions have emerged, policies have evolved, products and services have been designed to cope with the peculiar needs of the sector and priorities have changed with time. On top of that, technology has entered the space to alter the profile of financial services as never before. Policy making has generally been a function of time, place and person, other things remaining constant. At any given point in time, all different methods of providing financial services exist at different places. The field is so vast that there is room for all experiments and innovations to co-exist, from the traditional moneylender to sophisticated technology-driven institutions. While much development has taken place, there is need and scope to do so much more. The whole thing has largely been and continues to be a work in progress.

2

The Supply Push – Challenges of the Last Mile

ACCESS to financial services is as important in the rural sector as in the urban sector. Institutional finance in fact has been the single most important input for several enterprises in the rural sector, particularly agriculture. While the rural economy, much like the urban economy, comprises all income groups, the poor and not-so-poor, the rich and the enterprising, it is the poor segment which needs institutional finance the most. The poor, given their lack of assets or adequate financial resources to take care of their multifarious needs, including life cycle needs and emergent needs, have to manage whatever resource they have at their disposal. They save small amounts in their own way. They also take loans from within the family or community when they need more money. Both these things do, of course, have their limitations and cost. The cost associated with savings in the household in the form of cash can sometimes be enormous. We are all familiar with the usurious way the moneylenders and other entities in the informal sector operate. This is where the banking system, or for that matter any regulated institution providing financial services, is seen to play a role. There have been basically two approaches to institutional finance in the rural sector: one, under which the state mandates or facilitates provision of the services through mainstream institutions or other dedicated players; and two, where some service provider sees an opportunity or a market here and goes ahead to provide the needed service. Under both these approaches, similar type of products and services may be involved. The goal is the same but the end result and experience to the customer as well as the provider is vastly different.

Provision of financial services by mainstream banks and banks specifically set up for the purpose falls in the first category. Rural credit in India has been a story of state intervention from time to time. Starting with rural cooperatives, which were set up at the turn of the last century, we moved on to commercial banks and then had our dedicated players in the rural sector in the form of RRBs and local area banks. We established NABARD as the apex agriculture finance bank. We have moved on and established small finance banks and payment banks to further financial inclusion in the country. It has, thus, been a matter of continuous policy push-induced service provision in the rural sector. Several of these organisations, which were created, or asked to provide financial services and open outlets in the rural areas, have not generally seen this as a business opportunity, in the sense that given a choice, perhaps they would not have gone to those areas. There has been pressure on the banks from the government and the regulator to cater to the financial needs of the rural population and in the process they have been incentivised in some form if they conformed or penalised in some manner if they did not.

At the same time, there have also been players, including some banks and MFIs, which have seen this whole exercise as a business opportunity. We are talking of business opportunity and not a service motive, as a financial organisation like a bank or a non-banking financial company or even a cooperative society doing banking business must be viable in the process. Otherwise, we cannot expect it to provide financial services smoothly and consistently over a period of time. The government can always provide money to the needy in the form of a grant. However, there are two problems with this: first, the government just does not have the money to go on doing this indefinitely, especially when the number of people to be assisted in this manner is huge and there is a limit to taxation that a government can resort to; second, we cannot expect a society to forever depend on hand-outs, even if it is from the government. If it is going to progress, there must be proper livelihood development and imparting of entrepreneurial skills and opportunities to people to develop themselves. Hence, while the government can and does provide grants to the very poor in some cases, it has to be substantially supplemented with financial assistance from other institutions, which must be viably run to provide such services on a sustainable basis.

All over the world, whether in developing nations or in economically developed ones, support by the government to the disadvantaged groups in society has always been a policy focus. Inclusive growth has been a major policy plank in several countries and financial inclusion or the availability of institutional finance to all is ensured through conscious policy intervention at some stage. A quick recap of the developments in India would be in order.

The Cooperatives – People's Organisations

People's organisations have played a significant role in furthering the interests of the members in matters relating to economic activities, including finance. The cooperative credit structure in India is more than a century old[1] and enjoys a unique position in the rural credit delivery system with its vast network covering the remotest parts of the country. Cooperative Credit Institutions (CCI) are basically farmers' organisations set up primarily to meet the latter's credit-related requirements. Over a period of time, they have also provided other credit-linked services, such as supply of inputs, storage and marketing of produce, etc., thereby influencing the all-round development of agriculture and leading to improvement in the quality of life of villagers. The importance of cooperatives in dispensation of credit and allied services in rural areas has been emphasised time and again by several committees, right from the All India Rural Credit Survey Committee in the early 1950s, and the policies of RBI, NABARD and governments, both at the Centre and in the states, have been one of fostering the growth of the cooperative movement. Cooperatives have continued to play a crucial role in the rural credit scenario even after the entry of commercial banks and creation of RRBs with their vast rural branch network.

For historical reasons, two parallel wings of CCIs have come into existence and been developed; one for providing short-term and medium-term agricultural credit to farmers and the other for dispensing long-term credit, first for debt redemption and subsequently for investment in agriculture. The short-term credit structure obtaining in most parts of the country has been a federal one with a three-tier system, viz., State Cooperative Banks (SCBs) at the apex level in each state, District Central Cooperative Banks (DCCBs) at the district level, and Primary Agricultural Credit Societies (PACS) at the village level. In smaller states and Union Territories having a two-tier structure without the DCCBs, the credit requirements of the PACS are directly met by the SCBs. We have a formidable network of CCIs developed over the years. At the end of March 2016, there were 93,770 PACS, 370 DCCBs and 33 SCBs operating in the country[2].

The organisational structure of long-term cooperative credit is not of a uniform pattern all over the country. Known as Land Mortgage Banks (LMBs) in the early days, their name changed to Land Development Banks (LDBs) and subsequently to Agriculture and Rural Development Banks (ARDBs). While in some states, ARDB structure has a federal set up with the State Cooperative Agriculture & Rural Development Bank (SCARDB) at the state level and the affiliated Primary Cooperative Agriculture and Rural Development Banks (PCARDBs) at the district or *taluka* level, in some states, the structure is of a unitary type, with state-level ARDBs operating through their own branches. In some states, there is a mixed structure incorporating both the unitary and federal systems. For example, in Andhra Pradesh (and Telangana), an integrated structure providing all types of agricultural credit (both short-term and long-term) under the 'single window' credit system is prevalent, after the long-term structure was merged with the short-term structure in the mid-1980s. In smaller states, there is no separate long-term structure and the long-term credit needs are met by the State Cooperative Bank (SCB), together with other rural financial institutions. As of end-March 2016, there were 13 SCARDBs and 601 PCARDBs operating in the country[3].

SCBs and DCCBs being banks licensed under the Banking Regulation Act[4] have access to public deposits. While deposits constitute more than 50 per cent and 60 per cent of the total liabilities of the SCBs and DCCBs, respectively, PACS, which are technically not banks, depend mostly on borrowings from DCCBs. PACS can only collect deposits from members. There has been an increase in the deposits mobilised by PACS also in the recent years, inasmuch as the percentage of deposits to total resources of PACS constituted over 42 per cent at the end of March 2016[5].

Unlike SCBs and DCCBs, SCARDBs and PCARDBs depend heavily on borrowings (accounting for more than 80 per cent of their resources) primarily from NABARD, as they do not have access to public deposits except to a limited extent in the form of fixed deposits for a period of not less than 12 months, subject to aggregate deposits accepted and outstanding not exceeding the net owned funds. Although they carry the name of a bank, they are not banks in the conventional sense, as they do not take demand deposits from the public and do not come under the purview of the Banking Regulation Act, 1949. They are cooperative societies registered with the State Regulator.

Cooperative credit organisations in India have passed through several ups and downs and have, over a period of time, lost their prime role in purveying agricultural credit. They have been suffering from two major deficiencies – one, lack of sufficient funds, and two, lack of expertise and professionalism at the staff level. Their contribution in agricultural finance has steadily declined over the years. The share of cooperatives in the ground-level credit flow for agriculture and allied activities was 52 per cent in 1991-92; by 1996-97, it decreased to 44 per cent and continued to decrease. In 2016-17, it constituted 13 per cent of the total ground-level credit flow to agriculture. Barring a few pockets, their presence has become more of a burden than a true facilitator in the development process. How did this come about? While various committees have examined the issue from time to time and come out with several suggestions to tone up the system and to rid it of the ills that eat into the body fabric of cooperatives, it will be interesting to recall the origin of the cooperative structure in the country.

The cooperative movement in Europe and elsewhere was started by the people and they developed as truly member-controlled institutions, whereas in India, the cooperative credit system developed in response to government policy and was, as it were, superimposed from above on a society which was structurally different. The government's role in setting up and developing cooperative credit organisations was always overarching but became 'interference' after it started contributing towards the capital of the cooperatives since the mid-1950s, pursuant to the recommendation of the Rural Credit Survey Committee[6], about which we have discussed earlier in this chapter. Thereafter, the story of cooperative credit societies or cooperative banks has been one of relentless search for revival, search to find their feet in the complex web of political and administrative interference and a struggle to maintain their relevance in the face of sweeping changes in the banking landscape. Leadership in the cooperative banking sector has also failed to keep pace with time. It has wasted itself in the cobweb of operational details and survival needs and has not learned from the fast-paced developments in banking and finance that have impacted organisations everywhere, including the cooperatives themselves.

The latest and the most comprehensive report on restructuring the rural cooperative banking sector in India was submitted to the Government of India in 2005 by a committee headed by Prof A. Vaidyanathan, eminent agricultural economist and former member of the Planning Commission. The committee[7] recognised the need for government intervention to put CCIs back on the rails and recommended a package of measures in the areas of governance, law and operational matters relating to the rural cooperative credit system. The slew of measures was aimed at restoring the health of the three-tier cooperative system by looking at the tier at the bottom first – PACS and thereafter DCCBs and State Cooperative Banks in that order. The Central Government provided financial assistance to the tune of Rs 9,245 crore till June 2011 to implement the committee's recommendations. Other measures taken as part of the revival package included amendments of the State Cooperative Societies Acts, appointment of professional directors on the boards of the banks, statutory audit by chartered accountants, instead of the Cooperation Department of the state government and training of the personnel at various levels. Standardised accounting and MIS packages have been designed, and computerisation of DCCBs and PACS has been undertaken. However, there is still a lot to be done to address the issues that have crept into the system through years of neglect and unnecessary interference in their working. The originally planned member-driven institutions are now anything but member-driven. We are in a peculiar situation, where we have cooperatives, which are among the best, and also cooperatives, which are among the worst. To a large extent, it depends on the local leadership, which is responsible for the governance of cooperatives. Looking at the present state of these cooperative banks and societies in the country, one is forced to look back at what the Rural Credit Survey Committee had said in its report in 1954, 'Cooperation has failed, but cooperation must succeed'.

There have been problems on the regulatory front too. Being banks, they are regulated by the RBI but the supervision has been entrusted to NABARD. The major problem, however, arises from the fact that these banks are also cooperative societies and are set up under the Cooperative Societies Act of the state concerned. The state government also regulates them, in particular on matters relating to their registration, management, day-to-day administration and operation and, finally, liquidation. This has led to a situation where some state governments have issued guidelines to cooperative banks on their banking activities also, such as interest rates on loans. This duality of control has also prevented quick decision making in the cooperative banking system in the country, as the RBI had no jurisdiction on administrative and managerial matters in respect of these banks. Another issue was that the Banking Regulation Act, 1949 (as applicable to cooperative societies) did not apply to PACS or to any Primary Credit Society. As per the Act, a primary society can automatically convert to a cooperative bank, if it has banking as a main activity and has capital and reserves worth Rs 1 lakh only, an amount which was perhaps substantial when the law was enacted in the 1960s but is abysmally low by today's standards[8]. They are required to apply for licence to the RBI within three months of being eligible and can continue banking activities unless the licence application is rejected. This provision of law had led to the establishment of several cooperative banks over a period of time, which had applied for licence but the RBI had not taken any decision on licensing and had kept all these cases pending. These banks were, therefore, operating without any licence, unlike their counterparts in commercial banking. The continued operation of these banks was a threat to depositors' interest. For the common man it was difficult to differentiate between a licenced bank and a bank without licence. The RBI, though belatedly, took a decision to end this state of affairs and by March 2012, put in place a simplified licensing system for these banks. As a result, all SCBs, and all but three District Central Cooperative Banks in the country now stand licensed[9].

While the rural cooperative banking system developed in the country primarily due to policy initiatives of the government and with contribution to capital funds by the government, another segment of cooperative banks, known as Primary (Urban) Cooperative Banks, had started operating in urban areas, mainly driven by individual or community initiatives. As of March 2017, there were 1,562 such banks in the country, operating under licence from the RBI. Out of this, 1,083 banks had deposits of Rs 100 crore and above (called Tier II banks) and the remaining 479 had deposits of below Rs 100 crore (Tier I banks)[10]. These banks are mostly concentrated in some states, such as Gujarat, Maharashtra, Karnataka, Kerala, Andhra Pradesh and Telangana, where the cooperative movement was originally strong. This group of banks shows a high degree of heterogeneity. Those which are small in size mainly cater to the financial needs of an area or a community. Their portfolio shows that they provide financial assistance to mainly micro and small enterprises and other types of personal and small business loans to the middle class; some of them have also started giving loans for agriculture and related activities. Loans to micro and small enterprises constituted 28 per cent of the Urban Cooperative Banks' (UCBs) total credit as at March 2017, while lending to agriculture formed only 3 per cent of total credit[11]. Some of the UCBs are, however, fairly large; they operate in several states and are comparable in operations with commercial banks. A high-powered committee on UCBs set up by the RBI in 2015 (Chairman: R. Gandhi, then Deputy Governor) had observed that such large UCBs were losing their cooperative character and had recommended that corporatisation would be the best alternative for the large-sized UCBs.

Many of the UCBs, particularly those which are small in size, face serious governance issues. This sector has passed through several ups and downs. There have been cases of spectacular failures, such as The Madhavpura Mercantile Cooperative Bank in Gujarat, and the Charminar Cooperative Bank in Andhra Pradesh, which occurred in the first decade of the century. As in the case of RCBs, there is duality of control in these banks also, with the state government, through the Cooperation Department and the Registrar of Cooperative Societies, looking after the establishment, administrative and managerial aspects and closure and liquidation of the banks, and the RBI regulating the banking-related activities. The crisis faced by these banks showed that it was imperative for the RBI and state governments to work together in a coordinated manner. To address the issue of governance and operational viability faced by several of these banks, the RBI had entered into MoUs with state governments and set up a Task Force on Cooperative Urban Banks (TAFCUB) in the states, to jointly monitor the health of the banks at the state level and suggest appropriate action in case of weak banks. Mergers among urban banks have also been encouraged and some banks with serious problems have seen their banking licence cancelled and are facing liquidation. Experience shows that the TAFCUB mechanism has been fairly successful in addressing the challenges faced by the sector. It has been a practical approach to a highly complex issue of governance in cooperative banks.

Commercial Banks in Rural Finance

The first effort to involve a commercial bank in provision of rural credit dates back to 1955 with the conversion of the then Imperial Bank of India into State Bank of India (SBI) as recommended by the Rural Credit Survey Committee. The committee felt that with the growing financial needs of the agriculture sector, cooperative banks just did not have the resources to meet the needs and commercial banks had to be brought in to facilitate funds flow to agriculture. A programme of branch expansion in rural areas was undertaken with the SBI taking the lead and its associate banks (seven banks forming subsidiaries of SBI were nationalised in 1960) following suit. In terms of the Committee's recommendations, the SBI also started providing several financial facilities to cooperatives, including cooperative processing and marketing societies.

A multi-agency approach to rural credit delivery was also recommended by the Rural Credit Review Committee (July 1969), which observed that cooperatives had to be strengthened but also felt that farmers would be better served if other institutions co-existed with them in healthy competition.

A major push came in the wake of nationalisation of major commercial banks in 1969, which was to facilitate flow of bank credit to the hitherto neglected sectors of the Indian economy, particularly agriculture and small industries. At that time, within the government itself, there were many who opposed the outright nationalisation of banks but advocated greater control over the operations of banks. A scheme of social control over banks had been introduced in 1968, with the main objective of achieving a wider spread of bank credit, preventing its misuse, directing a larger volume of credit to the priority or neglected sectors and making the banking sector a more efficient instrument of economic development. However, the basic structure of banks and their way of functioning remained the same and the scheme of social control was not seen as being sufficient to make the commercial banking system a meaningful instrument of social change.

In a broadcast to the nation on the day 14 major banks (having minimum deposits of Rs 50 crore each) were nationalised in July 1969, the then Prime Minister Indira Gandhi stated that 'an institution such as a banking system, which touches—and should touch—the lives of millions, has necessarily to be inspired by social purpose and has to subserve national priorities and objectives.' The provision of finance through the banking system was, therefore, sought to be made an important driver of social change in the country. The very concept of sound banking business underwent a drastic change. Credit was no longer to be provided only to those who were in a position to furnish adequate security for loan, in terms of property or other assets. It was required to be provided to credit-worthy projects even in the absence of security. Significant changes in the banks' method of working and the attitudes of bank officials were called for to give effect to the far-reaching changes contemplated. Guidelines on priority sector lending and Lead Bank Scheme followed and the banking sector in the country was focused on achieving the lending targets. The issue of viability or profitability was not on the agenda of discussions. Six more commercial banks having minimum deposits of Rs 200 crore each were nationalised in 1980.

The nationalised banks tried to reach and finance farmers not only directly through their branches but also through primary cooperative societies. Under a scheme introduced in 1970, some PACS in the jurisdiction of weak DCCBs were ceded to commercial banks. Commercial banks also organised Farmers' Service Societies (FSS) and in tribal areas, Large Adivasi Multipurpose Societies (LAMPS). These initiatives, coupled with the Village Adoption Scheme developed by some banks, including the SBI, helped in reaching out to the farmers and those engaged in other related occupations in the rural sector.

Policy makers in India took a position to provide financial services in rural areas through the regular banking system although other types of finance providers, especially the non-banking financial institutions and several related entities (such as chit funds, cooperative societies, etc) did exist and continued to provide financial services in their own way. It was assumed that given the government mandate, banks (read commercial banks) would take all active steps in providing banking services in the hinterland. It did start with a bang immediately after nationalisation of major commercial banks in the country but it was done under pressure and appeared to be too costly and inconvenient for commercial banks to be continued forever. Especially in the wake of the focus on bank profitability that almost became a mantra for the banking system, to the exclusion of most other so-called socially relevant parameters, when the country adopted liberalisation of the banking and financial system in 1991. The main problem was lack of a proper business model. Whatever success was achieved, was due largely to the initiatives taken by committed individuals within banks, but the system as a whole helped little in developing a viable model of credit delivery. The little hope the banking system had to take their services to the last excluded person, was getting progressively more difficult in such a scenario. Banks had to depend on other players for meeting the last mile connectivity. The major challenge that remained on the supply side – of reaching out to the last mile – could be addressed only with the help of either specialised organisations that came to exist or individuals who could literally 'carry' the services to the doorstep of the customer.

A traditional criticism of commercial banks has been their general lack of understanding of the rural scenario, for which they were not able to develop products and services appropriate to the needs of low-income families in rural areas. In the initial days, they could perhaps have avoided this shortcoming by working in close coordination with the rural cooperative banking system. But that did not happen. With an expanding agricultural economy, there was scope for every institution to do business in the sector. Cooperative banks and commercial banks worked on the stand-alone basis and in their own different ways. Over a period of time, deficiencies in each of the two structures got amplified, so much so that the policy makers had to think of another set of institutions in the rural banking space, which would combine the best of the two sectors, avoiding those deficiencies.

The operations of commercial banks in rural areas have not been a smooth process and have passed through several vicissitudes. Once the euphoria associated with bank nationalisation was over, it became clear that public sector banks had swallowed much more than they could digest and urgent action was necessary to restore their health. Reforms in the banking sector became part and parcel of the liberalisation process undertaken in the early 1990s. Based on the far-reaching recommendations of the Committee on the Financial System (Narasimham Committee I), the government set out to improve the operational efficiency of commercial banks. Banks, which till then never thought of earning a profit in their rural operations, suddenly became aware that they had had to be profitable to ensure survival.

Sudden emphasis on profit earning left banks confused. The first casualty was of course rural banking. In the post-nationalisation set-up, regulation had also been appropriately tuned to the needs of the rural sector. One of the regulations that had a remarkable impact on the rural scene related to opening of branches of banks, known as the Branch Licensing Policy. The rule was that to be able to open one branch in an urban or a metropolitan area, a commercial bank had to open four branches in rural and semi-urban centres. This led to opening of branches without insisting on their viability over a period of time. But this forced expansion of the banking network in the rural sector was the first to suffer in the wake of the banking sector reforms. Rural branches of commercial banks which had increased from 1,441 in December 1969 to 35,216 in March 1991, declined to 30,760 as of March 2005[12]. The policy favoured reorganisation of bank branches through shifting or relocation, although closure of a single rural branch of a commercial bank was not allowed. The performance of commercial banks in lending to the priority sector, which included agriculture, small industries and a few other areas where bank credit was desirable but not forthcoming, also suffered as a result of the shifting perceptions. Banks' lending to the agriculture sector, as percentage of their net bank credit, declined from 14.8 in March 1991 to 12.5 in March 2005. A survey of Small Borrowal Accounts (SBAs) by the RBI shows that the number of SBAs declined from 6.25 crore as of March 1992 to 4.68 crore in March 1998[13]. Clearly, banks were re-defining their priorities.

After this jolt, affirmative action was necessary to continue with rural focus. The trend of declining branch network and percentage of agricultural advances to net bank credit, however, got reversed in the next decade, as the government and the Central Bank re-affirmed the commitment to the rural and priority sector lending by banks. As a result, rural branches of commercial banks increased to 38,982 in March 2016 and the share of agriculture in public sector banks' net bank credit also improved to 17 per cent in March 2015[14]. The number of SBAs also increased to 9.41 crore in March 2008. Although the multi-agency system comprising cooperative banks, commercial banks and RRBs continued in the rural space, aggressive branch opening and lending to agriculture by commercial banks resulted in the decline in the share of cooperative banks in the credit flow to the agriculture sector and a commensurate rise in the share of commercial banks, with RRBs more or less maintaining their share. The share of cooperative banks in agricultural finance stood at 17.5 per cent in 2015-16, which further decreased to 12.8 per cent in 2016-17, while commercial banks' share, which constituted 68.9 per cent in 2015-16, improved further to 76.4 per cent in 2016-17. RRBs, with more than 20,000 branches across the country, mainly in rural areas, contributed only 13.6 per cent to the agricultural credit flow in 2015-16 and it further declined to 10.8 per cent the next year[15].

The role of commercial banks in rural finance was further highlighted when financial inclusion was formally adopted as a policy focus in 2005. The idea was to bring the people, who for various reasons had not availed of banking facilities, into the fold of banking. It was consciously started as a bank-led process, as the policy makers wanted to leverage on our vast banking network in the country and the rich experience of our banking system in dealing with the poor. But to provide banking services, banks needed to set up branches or some other mode of servicing for rural areas, such as mobile vans, satellite offices, etc. These modes of operation were not popular. Branch banking was the preferred mode, even in the rural sector. This was, however, going to push up the cost of operations. Banks did not expect commensurate business generation at these unbanked and unserved rural centres, which they were required to service as part of the financial inclusion exercise. Banks clearly needed some support in reaching out to the rural hinterland and to reach out to the last mile, where they apparently did not see any 'fortune at the bottom of the pyramid'.

A major policy support came in January 2006, when the RBI issued guidelines for the appointment of Business Facilitators (BFs) and Business Correspondents (BCs) by banks for carrying out the financial inclusion agenda and provide doorstep banking services[16]. This was on the basis of recommendations made by the RBI Internal Group on Rural Credit and Microfinance, under the chairmanship of H. R. Khan, the then Principal of the College of Agricultural Banking, Pune, (who subsequently became Deputy Governor of the RBI) in 2005. The policy initiative provided a much needed support to the banking system which was all along struggling to deliver the last mile services in the hinterland, to the financially excluded persons. Business Facilitators were engaged to provide service to banks without handling cash at any stage, whereas BCs were involved in cash handling, in addition to other types of work which BFs were doing. Some banks were quick to recognise the opportunity, while others waited and watched but eventually all the existing banks, both in the public and private sectors, as also RRBs, started using BFs and BCs. The policy got fine-tuned several times, particularly with regard to the type of entities to be appointed as BCs and BFs and the delivery channels to be adopted. Starting with BCs appointed by banks themselves, it moved forward to appoint BCs through service providers, which meant banks were no longer directly associated with the appointment of BCs. The Department of Financial Services (DFS) under the Finance Ministry also added to the way service providers and BCs were appointed and the area of financial inclusion through BCs became a fertile ground for quick changes in policy and practices, so much so that all the modes of appointing BCs came to co-exist at any given point of time in several geographies, leading to some avoidable confusion. In spite of all this, the BC model had come to stay. People have seen its relevance in the context of financial inclusion and the term 'Business Correspondent' has become an accepted terminology in banking in India.

While initially it showed the promise of working quite well, both with banks and customers, the BC model later ran into operational difficulties. Limited experience with business models suitable for small value accounts and doorstep service delivery and lack of appreciation of alternative models resulted in the slow adoption of such mechanisms. With the entry of corporate BCs, i.e. BCs appointed by technology service providers and other corporate entities, with whom banks made arrangements, the issue of ownership had also emerged. The BC acted on behalf of a bank and the bank had a direct responsibility for the success or failure of the BC. Even then, in several cases, the sense of ownership was just not there, resulting in the BC not realising her true potential. Capacity building of BCs on a continuous basis was required, as was a suitable and regular remuneration to her. But then at the end of the day, everything was related to the fact that not many bankers were seeing the whole exercise making financial sense. Many did it under pressure without putting their hearts into it, and some others watched the show, as it were, from a distance, looking at the developments as they played out under the watchful, often interfering and always over-expectant eyes of the government and the regulator.

At the root of all this was the fact that perhaps we expected too much too quickly from this model. Systems take some time to develop and their acceptance by the society also takes time. The BC model was something the system was literally waiting for but the government as well as the regulator were committed to fast-tracking the financial inclusion process and any learning from experience had to be quickly translated to policy and scaled up. There was also the fact that the BC model had not been successfully implemented anywhere except Brazil. Even there, it was used mainly as a bill payment mechanism rather than as a tool to facilitate deposit and credit transactions with banks. Nowhere, therefore, was there a real business model appropriate to the relatively informal functioning of the micro-economy of low-income families; nowhere was there a holistic experience that the Indian banking system could turn to for guidance and reference while implementing the agency model through BCs. Viewed from another angle, this was perhaps an opportunity for India to provide a successful model to the world, which could then have been replicated elsewhere had all the stakeholders taken it in its true spirit.

However, the focus on financial inclusion and the implementation of the BC model has led to the establishment of a huge network of banking outlets in the six lakh plus villages of the country. One indication of the success of the exercise is that the total banking outlets in villages increased from 67,694 as of March 2010 to 2,00,760 as of March 2013 and further to 5,98,093 in March 2017. The latter comprised 50,860 rural branches, 5,43,472 BC outlets, and 3,761 other modes of extending banking services in villages[17].

Regional Rural Banks – Specialised Rural Banking Institutions

The rural credit policy in India has had at its core the twin goals of bringing an increasing number of people within the formal financial system and using credit as an instrument of poverty alleviation. Several measures have been taken by the Government of India and the RBI from time to time to achieve these goals. Even after commercial banks were brought into the field of rural banking in the post-nationalisation scenario to supplement the efforts of cooperatives, a large segment of the rural population remained outside the fold of banking services at that time. A working group constituted by the Government of India in 1975 under the chairmanship of M. Narasimham, former Governor of the RBI, to explore the possibilities of evolving an alternative rural credit agency, recommended the formation of a new set of regionally oriented rural banks, which would combine the local feel and familiarity characteristic of cooperatives and the professionalism and resource base of commercial banks. The new institutions were visualised as a hybrid of commercial and cooperative banks which would supplement the efforts of the existing rural financial institutions.

Following the recommendation and an ordinance issued by the Government of India, the first RRB in the country was set up in Moradabad district of Uttar Pradesh on 2 October, 1975. The bank, sponsored by Syndicate Bank, is still known as Prathama Bank. RRBs were sponsored by commercial banks, typically public sector banks, which held 35 per cent of the RRB share capital. The Central Government contributed 50 per cent of the share capital, with the remaining 15 per cent being contributed by the State Government under whose jurisdiction the RRB operated. By 1991, the number of RRBs in the country went up to 196. Only one RRB was established thereafter in the Union Territory of Pondicherry (Puduvai Bharathiar Grama Bank sponsored by Indian Bank) in 2008.

RRBs have a special place in the multi-agency approach adopted to provide agricultural and rural credit in India. These banks are state-sponsored, regionally based and rural-oriented. As enshrined in the Preamble to the RRBs Act, 1976, RRBs were established 'with a view to developing the rural economy by providing, for the purpose of development of agriculture, trade, commerce, industry and other productive activities in the rural areas, credit and other facilities, particularly to small and marginal farmers, agricultural labourers, artisans and small entrepreneurs and for matters connected therewith and incidental thereto.'

The story of RRBs in India is the story of misplaced expectations and a less than practical approach to policy. These small, localised banks were set up with a lot of expectations. They were supposed to combine the local feel and familiarity of cooperatives with the business strength of commercial banks and to be a low-cost institution, employing local resources, particularly human resources. But as subsequent developments have shown, this did not happen. Even the cost structure did not remain low, thanks to a ruling made by the National Industrial Tribunal in 1990, which ruled in favour of same pay for same work in the banking sector. This immediately pushed up the cost of operations of RRBs, without in any manner improving the work practices or even the scope for doing business with a semblance of viability. Although they were set up or sponsored by a commercial bank, usually a public sector bank, which was subsequently made accountable for the performance of the sponsored RRBs, it did not help matters much and as it turned out, the sponsor became in many cases a competitor of an RRB. Handholding sometimes gives an opportunity for arm twisting!

It has always been a matter of accepted wisdom that only a strong entity can help a weak entity and that to help the poor, an organisation need not itself become poor. But that is what actually happened in the case of our RRBs. In the process of providing financial services to the poor, they ended up becoming poor themselves. In 1996, out of 196 banks, only 45 were reported as profit making. This was mainly because of misplaced priorities, which never encouraged sound functioning of these institutions, but on the other hand, had all sorts of expectations from them and subjected them to experimentation at regular intervals. As aptly described by an RRB chairman, the hands and legs of these banks were tied and they were thrown into water, with the expectation that they would be able to smoothly swim back to the shore.

With the financial sector reforms in full swing in the early 1990s, the RRB sector could not remain a distant landscape. Sooner or later, the matter had to be sorted out. Thereafter, for a full decade, several policy measures were taken to improve the functioning of RRBs and to make their operations viable in the backdrop of increasing competition. It did show result. The number of profitable RRBs increased from 45 in the year 1996 to 148 in 2004. Such incremental effectiveness, however, had its limitations. Urgent action was needed if the system was to continue in a sustainable way. It fell on the shoulders of an Advisory Committee appointed by the RBI to chart a new path for these banks. In 2005, the Advisory Committee, set up to review the flow of credit to agriculture and related activities from the banking system (Vyas Committee, as it is popularly known), recommended the amalgamation of RRBs, state-wise and sponsor bank-wise. The government accepted it and, with support from all the stakeholders, took the process of reorganisation forward. The reorganisation was done in two phases. In the first phase, RRBs of the same sponsor bank in a state were amalgamated into a single entity and in the second phase, RRBs pertaining to different sponsor banks in a state were amalgamated. This process led the number of RRBs in the country to reduce from 196 to 56, which is continuing today. With liberalisation and deregulation and improving their scope of doing business, their financial shape improved and RRBs are now providing all the services that commercial banks provide, with the only limitations imposed by geography. They continue to be limited to a state or part thereof, which is a handicap they have to live with at least in the foreseeable future.

It is interesting to note that in spite of all these changes, the focus of the original law, which led to the establishment of RRBs, the RRBs Act, 1975, remains intact, so far as the objective and thrust of their operations are concerned. As per the Preamble to the Act, RRBs were set up for 'developing the rural economy by providing, for the purpose of development of agriculture, trade, commerce, industry and other productive activities in the rural areas, credit and other facilities, particularly to the small and marginal farmers, agricultural labourers, artisans and small entrepreneurs and for matters connected therewith and incidental thereto.' As per the Act, they are still expected to provide financial services only to the weaker sections of the society, whereas in reality, they have moved beyond that mandate. Occasionally, this creates a flutter in the meetings of some forums or the pages of some reports and publications, but the banks have learnt to move on. The overriding consideration has been ensuring viability of operations. Even the heads of these banks are evaluated annually on the basis of a set of performance parameters in which profitability plays an important part.

As per NABARD data, 50 out of 56 RRBs earned profit during 2015-16 and 45 out of 56 banks were sustainably viable, i.e. earning profits and carrying no accumulated losses[18]. Although several RRBs are showing good operational results and some are actually making a difference in the areas they are servicing, many RRBs still suffer from the 'weakness syndrome'. Despite earning profits year after year, they continue to feel that they are small and weak institutions in need of continuous support. Several RRBs sincerely believe that continuous handholding is necessary to ensure their functioning. This attitude has prevented many of these banks from putting forth their best and has, in fact, not brought in the necessary competition that they were supposed to pose to other operators, mainly commercial banks in the rural sector. A manifestation of the poor image of these banks is the reluctance of government agencies to park their funds in RRBs in spite of the fact that they are created and predominantly owned by the government, both Central and state. Therefore, in spite of its potential to finance a larger proportion of rural development activities, the RRB sector remains highly under-utilised even today.

NABARD – Setting up an Apex Bank

The RBI had set up a committee in March 1979 under the chairmanship of B. Sivaraman to review the arrangements for institutional credit for agriculture and rural development. The committee, better known by its acronym CRAFICARD, submitted an interim report in November 1979 and the final report in January 1981. In its interim report, the committee recommended the setting up of NABARD as the apex bank for overseeing rural and agricultural credit system in the country. Details of the new institution were outlined in the final report. Accordingly, the NABARD Bill was passed in the Parliament in December 1981 and NABARD was established in July 1982, taking over the Agriculture Refinance and Development Corporation (ARDC), a subsidiary of the RBI and its Agricultural Credit Department (ACD). The mandate given by the NABARD Act was to provide and regulate credit and other facilities for the promotion and development of agriculture, small-scale industries, cottage and village industries, handicrafts and other rural crafts and other allied economic activities in rural areas with a view to promoting integrated rural development and securing the prosperity of rural areas.

Before the establishment of NABARD, the RBI, by virtue of its mandate enshrined in the Reserve Bank of India Act 1934, was entrusted with the responsibility of overseeing, coordinating and facilitating the flow of rural credit. In fact, this was a unique developmental role being played by the RBI in a striking contrast to the working of other central banks, something which continues even to this day. While the basic thrust of NABARD as enshrined in the Act remains the same, its operating field has been widened from time to time, in the context of developments taking place in the rural economy, the priorities of the successive governments and its own operational imperatives.

The three pillars, viz., financial, supervisory and developmental functions, continue to define the activities of NABARD, with all three gaining importance with the passage of time. The NABARD (Amendment) Act, 2017, which came into effect in January 2018, has increased the share capital of NABARD from Rs 5,000 crore to Rs 30,000 crore, with provision to increase it further with the concurrence of the RBI. At present, the entire share capital of NABARD is vested with the Government of India. At the time of establishment, NABARD had taken over two funds from the RBI, the National Rural Credit (long-term operations) Fund and the

National Rural Credit (Stabilisation) Fund. The first aimed at providing long-term finance to the cooperative sector and the second assisted conversion of short-term loans into medium-term loans when natural calamities occurred. Several dedicated funds have been established with NABARD over time to provide financial support to a number of activities, such as building rural infrastructure including warehouses, watershed development, development of cooperatives, food processing, development of RRBs, ensuring financial inclusion and literacy, etc. The funding of several of these funds is done by channelising the shortfall in priority sector lending of commercial banks about which we have discussed earlier and which we shall focus a little more in the chapter on policy making. In fact, as per the Annual Report of NABARD, during 2017, the single major source of funds for NABARD (constituting 30.29 per cent of total funds) was the deposits made by banks in the Rural Infrastructure Development Fund (RIDF).

The supervisory functions of NABARD extend over the rural cooperative banking set-up and RRBs. The importance of this role has been accentuated in the context of consolidation of RRBs, which has made them much bigger than originally planned, and the problems constantly faced by cooperative banks, both short-term and long-term, in ensuring viable operations and good governance. NABARD has been striving to strengthen its supervisory capabilities, with the scope and complexities of operations of these banks increasing manifold. There have been recommendations by some committees to shift the supervisory function to the RBI, keeping in view the fact that all RRBs, as also several SCBs are included in the Second Schedule to the RBI Act, 1934 (they are Scheduled Banks). However, the status quo continues.

Most important has been the developmental function of NABARD. In a developing country like ours, continuous innovations are necessary for reaching out to the last mile, efficiently and effectively. Here, NABARD has quite a few achievements to be proud of, particularly the SHG-Bank Linkage Programme, the Kisan Credit Card Scheme, operationalisation of the RIDF, the Farmers Club Programme (which emanated from the Vikas Volunteer Vahini programme undertaken by NABARD in its early days), etc. NABARD's increasing involvement in improving the credit absorption capacity in the rural sector, the function of which is to improve capital formation in agriculture, has been eluding the system in spite of several steps taken by the government and NABARD. Increasing farmers' income, which is a policy thrust under the present government at the Centre, is going to be of paramount importance in the times to come. NABARD's achievements are going to be evaluated mainly on these parameters. NABARD's strong human resource base will be increasingly called upon to strategise these objectives and to take the right initiatives so as to make these strategies implementable. While there can be different views on the conflicts inherent in the three functions of NABARD, it must use its regulatory and supervisory role for strengthening its developmental objectives.

The Lead Bank Scheme

The committee on the organisational framework for the implementation of social objectives under the chairmanship of Prof D. R. Gadgil, set up by the National Credit Council in 1968, had recommended the adoption of an area approach for bridging the spatial and structural credit gaps in the country. Post-nationalisation, another committee headed by F. S. Nariman (known as the Bankers Committee) further examined the matter and concluded that districts would be the unit for the area approach. Each district would be allotted to a bank, which would perform the role of a lead bank in the district. Accordingly, the Lead Bank Scheme (LBS) was introduced by the RBI in December 1969. The scheme aims at coordinating the activities of banks and other developmental agencies through various forums to achieve the objective of enhancing the flow of bank finance to the priority sector and to promote the role of banks in the overall development of the rural sector. For coordinating the activities in the district, a particular bank is assigned the Lead Bank (LB) responsibility of the district. The LB, which has the privilege of being the first among equals, is expected to assume leadership role for coordinating the efforts of credit institutions and the government in planning and monitoring the flow of credit and related activities. Banks and the government meet periodically, at least once every quarter, at the block, district and state level. Credit plans are prepared at the district level and then aggregated at the state level in the form of a State Credit Plan. Every quarter in the meetings of the Block Level Bankers Committee (BLBC), the District Consultative Committee (DCC) and the State Level Bankers Committee (SLBC), performance of banks in achieving the credit targets is discussed threadbare in the presence of government officials at the appropriate levels. The Government also takes this opportunity to review the performance of various bank credit-linked programmes. Other issues of mutual interest are also flagged in these meetings, to which various other institutions are invited as per requirement.

In 1989, the Service Area Approach (SAA) was dovetailed into the LBS, and under this, every rural and semi-urban branch of a public sector bank was allotted a service area within which it was its responsibility to extend priority sector loans. The SAA also came bundled with branch-level planning for credit, which would be aggregated at the block level, then at the district level. A person residing in the service area of a bank branch was required to approach that branch for loan. If for any reason, he had to approach any other branch of any bank, a no-due certificate was needed from the service area branch. Although initially, when it was a matter of gaining access to a bank branch which was not available earlier, there was some logic in allocating service areas among bank branches and making a branch responsible to lend in its service area, soon it became clear that the mechanism actually proved too restrictive and customers were forced to deal with one particular branch, irrespective of whether it was able to take care of their requirements or not. Further, with the liberalisation of economy, it was clearly not desirable to stifle competition in providing services in the rural sector. Banks, which were more aggressive in expanding their outreach in the rural sector, found themselves handicapped by the SAA. In due course, therefore, the SAA was abolished (2005), except for lending under various government-sponsored schemes, for which clear responsibility was required to be assigned to bank branches.

Over the years, the focus of the LBS has shifted to inclusive growth and financial inclusion. The Scheme was last revisited in 2009 by a high-level committee set up by the RBI (Chairman: Usha Thorat, then Deputy Governor). The committee suggested widening the scope of the scheme and redefining the focus on financial inclusion. The use of information technology (IT) and intermediaries had enabled banks to increase outreach, scale and depth of banking services at affordable cost. SLBC Convenor Banks at the state level and LBs in districts are required to focus on the need for achieving total financial inclusion through provision of banking services in rural areas. Such banking services may not necessarily be extended through a brick and mortar branch but can be provided through any of the various forms of ICT-based models, including through BCs.

Lack of digital connectivity in rural areas, though a major impeder to financial inclusion in the country, obviously cannot be an excuse for not pursuing financial inclusion by banks. SLBC Convenor Banks have the responsibility to take up with state governments such issues of physical and digital connectivity, conducive law and order situation, uninterrupted power supply and adequate security, etc. for ensuring banking expansion to all unbanked centres, where penetration by the formal banking system is required.

The LBS has been a unique experiment in India for bringing together the two major stakeholders in the development process, viz., banks and the government, which jointly plan and monitor the process of development finance. Of course, the government and banks are different entities, having their own priorities. They seldom arrive at a consensus on any difficult issue but at least the scheme provides a forum where both can sit and discuss and try to find a solution. Development requires continuous coordination among all the stakeholders and in a democratic country like ours, continuous dialogue among them is the only way to take the development process forward. On its part, the LBS can be successful only if both the government and banks take it seriously, understand and appreciate its uniqueness and act in accordance with its spirit. There are many local level issues to which solutions can be found locally if one is sincere and puts one's best foot forward. For such entities, the LBS provides the most appropriate framework within which many inter-organisational issues having impact on the development process can be effectively addressed.

Local Area Banks – Rural Banks in Private Sector

The push towards liberalisation and privatisation in the 1990s also to some extent impacted the rural financial sector, when the Government of India announced in 1996 the setting up of local banks in the private sector, covering a few districts in analogy with RRBs, for supplementing the existing structure in providing financial services in rural India. It may be noted that from time to time, policy makers have toyed with the idea of having more small banks in the country to take care of rural finance, as it is generally believed that small banks, which are locally based and familiar with local situations, would be in a better position to understand the financial needs of rural people and to design appropriate products suitable for their needs. In other words, these banks would entirely focus on rural finance, which in itself was a huge challenge. That's how RRBs came into existence. That is why it was thought that the private sector participation in this initiative would also be welcome. The then Finance Minister, delivering the budget speech in July 1996, said, 'It has been agreed with RBI to promote the setting up of new private Local Area Banks (LABs) with jurisdiction over two or three contiguous districts. This would enable the mobilisation of rural savings by local institutions and at the same time, make them available for investments in the local areas.'[19]

The experiment, which was at that time thought to help put in place a strong and viable rural banking structure, however, did not prove successful. The RBI did receive more than 200 applications (227 over a span of four and a half years).[20] However, the RBI stopped issuing any licence to set up LABs after 2002, acting on recommendations made by a committee it set up to review their performance. LABs, which were expected to act as RRBs in the private sector, did not fulfil that expectation. The net result was that after about two decades, (in 2016) only four LABs were operating in the country and as such, they did not have any appreciable impact on the delivery of financial services in the rural sector. In fact, all of them were operating in relatively well-banked and progressive states such as Andhra Pradesh, Telangana, Punjab and Maharashtra. One of these banks (in Punjab) has since been converted into a Small Finance Bank, while the remaining three play only a limited role in bringing about financial inclusion in the country.

Small Finance Banks and Payment Banks – The New Players

The search for an appropriate institutional set-up for rural finance continued beyond the establishment of LABs. The report of the Committee on Financial Sector Reforms (2008), chaired by Dr Raghuram Rajan, then Professor at University of Chicago, Booth School of Business, who subsequently became the Governor of the RBI, dwelt on the institutional arrangement and came out with a recommendation to set up more small banks in the private sector to further financial inclusion in the country. The Committee noted that instead of the large bank-led, public sector-dominated, mandate-ridden, branch expansion-focused strategy for inclusion, small local banks with low cost and efficient structures would work better[21]. However, the experience of LABs in the country, which was too fresh in memory, did not support such a policy prescription at that time. When Dr Rajan became the Governor of the RBI, it was an opportunity for him to plan the implementation of the earlier recommendation. A committee, set up by the RBI under the chairmanship of Dr Nachiket Mor, a member of the Central Bank's Board (Committee on Comprehensive Financial Services for Small Businesses and Low Income Households), recommended a differentiated banking system, with functionally specialised banks operating alongside full service banks. This sowed the seeds of the Payment Banks and the Small Finance Banks (SFBs).

The stated objective of setting up SFBs is furthering financial inclusion by providing savings vehicles primarily to the unserved and underserved sections of the population and supplying credit to small business units, small and marginal farmers, micro and small industries and other unorganised sector entities, through high technology-low cost operations. SFBs can also undertake other non-risk sharing simple financial services activities, not requiring any commitment of own fund, such as distribution of mutual fund units, insurance products, pension products, etc., with the prior approval of the RBI and after complying with the requirements of the sectoral regulators for such products. In view of the objective for which a SFB is set up, it is required to extend 75 per cent of its Adjusted Net Bank Credit (ANBC) to the sectors eligible for classification as Priority Sector Lending (PSL) by the RBI (as against 40 per cent applicable to commercial banks and 60 per cent to RRBs). While 40 per cent of its ANBC should be allocated to different sub-sectors under the PSL as per the extant prescriptions, the bank can allocate the balance 35 per cent to any one or more sub-sectors under the priority sector, where it feels it has competitive advantage.

The maximum loan size and investment limit exposure to a single and group obligor would be restricted to 10 per cent and 15 per cent of its capital funds, respectively. Further, to ensure that the bank extends loans primarily to small borrowers, at least 50 per cent of its loan portfolio should constitute loans and advances of up to Rs 25 lakh. After the initial stabilisation period of five years and after a review, the RBI said it might relax the above exposure limits.

All the 10 SFBs, which were given in-principle approval by the RBI, have started functioning. It is interesting to note that eight out of 10 were microfinance institutions (MFIs), which got converted to banks. With their deep understanding of the rural sector and innovative approach to finance, these banks are expected to bring the much desired nimbleness into the banking system and to make a difference in the lives of people.

It is well recognised that there is a continuing need for transactions and savings accounts for the underserved in the population. Also, remittances have both macro-economic benefits for the region receiving them, as well as micro-economic benefits to the recipients. Higher transaction costs of making remittances diminish these benefits. Several studies have highlighted the difficulties faced by migrant workers in various places in the country in sending money to their families and the role played by informal sector agencies in the absence of any effective access to the formal banking system. The primary objective of setting up Payments Banks (PBs) was to further financial inclusion by providing small savings accounts (up to Rs 1 lakh) and payments/remittance services to the migrant labour workforce, low income households, small businesses, other unorganised sector entities and other users, by enabling high volume-low value transactions in deposits and payments/ remittance services in a secured technology-driven environment. A PB, however, cannot undertake lending activities. Although initially, several entities had expressed enthusiasm to set up such banks, because of the restrictive business model, many have started expressing doubts about their long-term sustainability. As against in-principle approval given by the RBI to set up 11 banks, three have subsequently withdrawn and of the remaining eight, only five PBs have started operation. Only time will tell in what manner and to what extent these banks will contribute to the process of financial inclusion in the country, especially in the rural sector. Expectations from the PB set up by India Post are very high in view of the vast network of post offices which already exist throughout the country and the services being provided by the Post Office Savings Bank, especially in the rural sector.

The banking scenario in the country, seen in the context of rural banking, presents an evolving picture, with major part of it already stabilised, while a part of it is yet to find its grip. With financial inclusion being seen as a major challenge to the banking system in this country and the gap in providing banking services estimated to be still very wide, policy favours a multiplicity of players co-existing in this field and the belief is that all initiatives are welcome. As the financial sector forges ahead to meet the challenges of the last mile, sometimes one wonders whether developments in the real economy are able to keep pace with developments in the financial sector and whether by merely making banking services available in our rural areas and not matching them with infrastructure and other facilities for sustainable livelihoods would really help the people realise their true potential.

Non-Banking Financial Companies (NBFCs) – Strong Support in Niche Areas

Non-banking financial activity is recognised as an integral part of the financial system in India as it complements commercial banking. Non-Banking Financial Companies (NBFCs) are active in certain niche areas, such as personal finance, tractor financc, SME finance, etc., and in certain pockets of the country. NBFCs can be advantageous due to their ability to lower transaction costs, quick decision making capabilities, customer orientation and prompt provision of services in certain segments. The absence of formal banking presence in a large number of villages also provided growth impetus to this sector and in the process all types of players emerged. The sector went into some kind of disrepute after it was discovered that the activities of a few very well-known entities in the sector were unlawful. In fact, these developments prompted the RBI to put in place comprehensive regulatory standards for the sector, which was till then not properly regulated. Given the profile of the sector, it is also recognised that appropriate vigilance and due diligence are needed to regulate this sector.

Traditionally, the objective of NBFC regulations was predominantly to protect the interests of depositors. However, as NBFCs grew in size and their interconnectedness with the banking system became visible and raised concerns about their capacity to disturb systemic stability, NBFCs were brought under prudential regulatory framework from 2006 onwards. The RBI has classified varieties of specific types of NBFCs separately and regulates each type differently. These include asset financing, core investment, loan, investment, micro-financing, factoring, infrastructure financing and mortgage guarantee activities. Further, in the case of housing finance, insurance and collective investment activities, which are statutorily defined as non-banking financial activities, their regulations have been left in the hands of other sectoral regulators such as the National Housing Bank (NHB), the Insurance Regulatory and Development Authority (IRDA), the Pension Fund Regulatory and Development Authority (PFRDA) and the Securities and Exchange Board of India (SEBI). This approach reflects the position that the non-banking financial system may contribute to financial deepening in these identified segments.

Nevertheless, the business model of NBFCs is inherently prone to risk. In November 2014, the RBI undertook a detailed review of the entire regulatory framework for the NBFC sector, with a view to transitioning, over time, to an 'activity-based regulation' of NBFCs, as against the existing approach of 'entity-based regulation'. The focus has been on addressing risks where they exist, addressing gaps in regulation, reducing complexities and making regulations simple and easy to follow, harmonising regulations within the sector and with that of banks to a limited extent, acknowledging that there may be pockets within the sector that do not require to be stringently regulated and giving adequate time to NBFCs to adjust to the revised regulatory framework, so that there are no disruptions in business. There are two broad categories of NBFCs requiring closer attention of regulators. The first set comprises non-deposit accepting NBFCs with asset size of less than Rs 500 crore, and the second set comprises non-deposit accepting NBFCs with assets of Rs 500 crore and above and deposit accepting NBFCs[22]. Reporting and regulatory provisions are accordingly applied to have a better focus on systemically important entities.

NBFCs depend to some extent on bank finance to carry on their activities. In fact, lending by commercial banks to NBFCs for on-lending to NBFCs is treated as part of their priority sector lending in the segment concerned, such as agriculture, MSME and microfinance depending on the activity NBFCs engaged in.

Microfinance – The Poor are Bankable

At the same time when banks were being pushed, cajoled, and compelled for offering financial services in the rural sector, particularly to the poor and excluded persons, the poor continued to get the services they needed, in the same village or town, albeit at a much higher cost and at a higher risk. The risk was in the case of default. Whatever asset she had was liable to be taken away if money was not repaid. Worse, in many cases, the borrower and her family lost their social standing and frequently ended up as bonded labourers, sometimes for generations.

In this backdrop, savings and credit groups as also cooperatives emerged in different parts of the world as effective solutions for helping people manage their financial needs. Cooperatives soon became another institutional structure and were subjected to several regulations by the government. The story of cooperative societies in India has been described above briefly. The informal associations of people, in whatever name called, grew parallel to the formal credit structure mainly to deal with their emergent needs.

The development of 'microcredit' in Bangladesh by Prof Muhammad Yunus and the establishment of Grameen Bank showed to the world that the poor were bankable, given the right financing model and close support and monitoring by the lending institution. In the words of Prof Yunus, 'People were not poor because they were stupid or lazy. They worked all day long, doing complex physical tasks. They were poor because the financial institutions which could help them widen their economic base simply did not exist in their country. It was a structural problem not a personal one'[23]. Not only did Grameen Bank provide micro loans to the poor, it also helped build a broader enabling and sustaining environment. Other institutions, mostly in the non-government sector, also came up in Bangladesh (BRAC, ASA, etc.) using some variant of the Grameen model of microcredit. Soon the model attracted worldwide attention. Experiments and pilot programmes were started in India too, to replicate the model as also to develop suitable methods to take advantage of the local situation in the country. The Bangladesh experience showed that women were better financial managers and that poor women had the capacity to take loans and repay in time. This led to the whole microfinance concept to be mostly women-centric, although groups comprising male members and those having mixed membership are also seen.

One such pilot project started by NABARD with the help of MYRADA in Karnataka, led to the development of the Self Help Group (SHG) model in India in the 1980s. The SHG was visualised as a homogeneous group of persons, from similar economic background and bound by common interests, coming together for some specific purpose. It was a micro-level socio-economic structure, which promoted self-help and mutual help, the same fundamental principle on which cooperatives were once established. While the SHG could be organised for any purpose, it was soon seen as a useful model for providing financial services, both saving and credit. It was a savings-first approach. Members of the group were required to contribute small amounts regularly to build up a common fund, which would later be utilised for internal lending to the needy members. This is what a self-sufficient SHG would go on doing. This was also seen as preparatory to get loans from banks, loans being given to the group as a whole with the understanding that it would pass on the loans to the members who required them. The group also performed partly the work of a bank, in the sense that monitoring, follow-up and recovery of loans was not required to be done directly by banks. It was done by SHGs. Each group was managed by a few members who had the necessary qualities. The model looked so attractive that when the programme started as a pilot, the banking regulator intervened to allow opening of bank accounts by these 'informal' groups, as SHGs were not registered under any law and were, therefore, not required to be regulated by anybody. The informal status helped them. Compliance to some existing law would have killed their spontaneity, and the growth of the SHG programme would probably have been stalled in the beginning itself.

SHG-Bank Linkage Programme

The SHG-Bank Linkage Programme (SHG-BLP), which started in 1991-92, has completed 25 years of operation and has changed the face of rural banking in the country. There have been several studies on the effectiveness of the programme, its contribution to social and financial progress of members, and its strengths and weaknesses.

Starting with a pilot programme of linking 500 SHGs with banks, it has grown over the years to more than 8.7 million SHGs linked to banks as in March 2017, with about 130 million members, most of whom (about 90 per cent) are women[24]. This has been recognised as the largest microfinance programme in the world.

Acting as conduits of bank credit, the SHGs which had around 10 to 20 members, performed their task quite well in the initial years. The membership of a group had to be restricted to 20, as otherwise provision of the Indian Companies Act, 2013 would have to be followed and the group had to be registered, robbing it of its informal character. The pilot project was soon followed by mainstreaming of the SHG-Bank Linkage Programme in 1996, and both NABARD and RBI pro-actively facilitated and actively monitored the developments.

Any programme in the socio-economic sphere, as successful as the SHG-BLP, spreading over the length and breadth of the country, was sure to attract the attention of the government. The government is primarily responsible for the development process, whether social or economic, and any action by any other agency in this domain would have to take this fact into account. The win-win situation for banks and SHG members, in which loans were availed of by poor persons through the group mechanism and repayment was taken care of by the SHGs, brought the government into the picture. In some states, the Government itself became the facilitator, while poverty alleviation programmes implemented by the Central as well as some state governments came to be focused on the SHG mode of delivery. Several private players, the MFIs, also came up to fill the gap between demand and supply of credit, using either the SHG model or the more ubiquitous Grameen Bank model to provide microcredit to the poor.

With the passage of time, the SHG-BLP, which once rested on the twin pillars of no-default and no-transaction cost for banks, has started showing cracks, as overdue and non-performing assets

(NPAs) have increased in several places. To be fair to them, SHGs cannot be expected to remain mute spectators, when waiver of various loans, especially agricultural loans, are routinely demanded and regularly allowed by state governments, and even the Government of India has announced a couple of agricultural loan waivers in the past. All this has almost killed the credit culture in the country. The repayment of SHG loans has also been affected.

SHGs have, however, played a more prominent role in the field of social mobilisation and social uplift of women than in the area of assisting members to obtain financial services and build up livelihoods. Being a member of an SHG has imparted confidence to the village women, who had doubly suffered for long for being women and for being poor. In the early days of implementation of the programme, loans of much smaller amounts were typically taken for consumption purposes. As the financial management capacity of SHGs improved and members started taking up livelihood activities with support from the SHG and from financing banks, the quantum of loan also increased, and many SHG women took up viable economic activities. But in spite of all this, the social (and political) impact of the SHG movement has been noteworthy.

The programme has raised a lot of hopes and expectations in the country and in almost all states, the governments have recognised the potential of SHGs in furthering not only financial inclusion but also in carrying forward many other activities. Thousands of women's groups in rural as well as urban areas constitute a formidable force, not only politically but also for governance purposes. That's how we see SHGs dealing with adult literacy in some states, healthcare in others, and in some others, helping the government in the procurement of agricultural produce. The flip side is that this overuse of SHGs has to some extent robbed them of their original informal character and diluted the focus on financial awareness and independence that the movement had set out to achieve.

The issue of NPAs in SHG-BLP has been discussed earlier in this chapter. The interesting point is that NPAs are not uniform everywhere in the country. They are seen only in some areas and are also institution-specific[25]. While some reasons, such as erosion of repayment climate, over-burdening of SHGs with all types of work, failure of crops when loans are related to agricultural activities, mishaps in the family, etc., can be common, there can be area-specific causes of NPAs, which would need a detailed study. Apart from NPAs, another long-standing issue relates to uneven spread of microfinance among states and regions. The southern part of the country has been the prime mover in microfinance, both the SHG-BLP and the MFI models, while other less developed states and areas have registered slow progress. Spread of microfinance is very slow in the states which needed it the most, such as the North-Eastern states, Bihar, Madhya Pradesh and Chhattisgarh. One reason could be the enthusiasm exhibited by the state government concerned. Those states, such as the southern states, where state governments are active players or promoters in the field of microfinance, have shown remarkable progress. Because microfinance intersects the development domain, the role of state governments is extremely important. In the absence of that support and encouragement, formal or informal, neither banks nor MFIs can achieve any significant level of success in this area.

One reason why SHG-BLP or for that matter other forms of microfinance flourished in the southern states could be the proactive nature of state governments. The other reasons are high level of financial literacy of the people and the generally higher level of economic development in these states. An interesting example would be the setting up of a cooperative society by the Government of Andhra Pradesh (then undivided) in 2011 to exclusively focus on financing of SHGs. Named Stree Nidhi, the society which has as members the SHG Federations of the state, also accesses bank loans for on-lending to the member federations, which further on-lend to the groups.

Microfinance Institutions (MFIs)

MFIs operated in the same field as the government and banks, and had the same target group. They were, however, generally more profit-oriented and the sector expanded rapidly, given their aggressive lending strategies and favourable incentive structure to induce the staff into pushing hard. The sector, which started operating in India in the mid-1990s, was quick to seize the opportunity and underwent tremendous accelerated growth. Between 2004 and 2009, the microfinance sector recorded a rapid growth, with CAGR of 86 per cent in loan portfolio and 96 per cent in borrowers[26]. The high growth made it a potential investment option with commercial investors. Investments increased by about US $ 380 million during the period 2004 to 2009, with almost 88 per cent of this flowing in the last two years of this period[27]. This was being described as the commercialisation of microfinance.

MFIs were, however, a mixed group; apart from NBFCs, which specialised in microfinance, MFIs also comprised societies, trusts, not-for-profit companies, and cooperatives, which were established under separate legal frameworks (Societies Registration Act, Indian Trust Act, Companies registered under Section 8 of the Companies Act, 2013, and State Cooperative Societies Act) as non-profit organisations and were responsible to their respective registering authorities. While the smaller among them were confined to some localities, the larger MFIs, which were also NBFCs, acquired nationwide presence.

It is one thing to make available financial services, especially loans, to the poor, it is another thing to push loans down their throat. The needs of the poor are so many and the availability of finance so limited and so irregular that inducing them to take a loan is not generally very difficult, especially when their financial literacy level is also low. As we have repeatedly seen, rapid expansion of MFIs' portfolio was often not accompanied by commensurate improvement in capacity building of the field staff in creating awareness among customers, and in monitoring the end use of loans by borrowers. The result has generally been lack of prudence in lending by some MFIs and an increase in indebtedness at the ground level, with sometimes a person borrowing from Peter to pay Paul.

This has admittedly been the darker side of microfinance and MFIs, which, driven by profit ushered in this era of uncertainty and not only suffered themselves but also brought disrepute to the entire sector. That the system had reached its limit and amendments were needed urgently, was obvious when in Krishna district of Andhra Pradesh, a government official issued orders in 2006 to close down the offices of a prominent MFI, citing usurious lending and unhealthy recovery practices to justify the action. Although this immediately led to some coordinated action on the part of the stakeholders and a code of conduct was evolved by Sa-Dhan, a network of MFIs, the system did not learn much from this development and the story became even more murky, leading to the Government of Andhra Pradesh to issue an ordinance in October 2010, bringing MFI operations in the State under government control and restricting operations of MFIs in the State[28]. It has often been called the 'Microfinance Crisis', but in reality, the development has negatively affected the working of MFIs in the State, even as the SHG-BLP continues to flourish, with the government continuing to play an active role in the promotion and practice of microfinance in the State (now bifurcated).

Several MFIs, which suffered due to the crisis in Andhra Pradesh, have since bounced back and have been registering reasonable progress in states other than Andhra Pradesh and Telangana, and quite a few have also started registering pre-crisis levels of growth and expansion of portfolio. The major difference now is that the RBI has become an active regulator of NBFC-MFIs, a separate category of NBFCs designated after the crisis, which called for focused regulation of the sector. This was based on the recommendations of a sub-committee of the RBI Central Board of

Directors chaired by Y. H. Malegam, Member of the Board. The sub-committee set up to study the issues and concerns in the MFI sector, submitted its report in January 2011. For the first time, permitted activities of these NBFC-MFIs were spelt out clearly. At least 85 per cent of their assets were required to be in the nature of qualifying assets, which meant loans given to people subject to specified parameters. The parameters included the borrower's annual household income cap of Rs 60,000 in rural areas and Rs 1,20,000 in urban areas; loan amount cap of Rs 35,000 in the first cycle; and Rs 50,000 in the second cycle and total indebtedness cap for the borrower at Rs 50,000. The tenure of loans was to be a minimum of 24 months for loans exceeding Rs 15,000 and all loans were required to be extended without any collateral. An aggregate margin cap of 12 per cent was specified till March 2014, after which the margin cap for large MFIs (assets exceeding Rs 100 crore) was to be 10 per cent, while for other small MFIs, the cap was retained at 12 per cent. For the first time in the history of Indian microfinance, a clear regulatory map had been designed for the larger players, NBFC-MFIs. Although for some time, the sector itself was clamouring for regulation, preferably by the RBI, it was not until the MFI crisis played out in Andhra Pradesh that the RBI set up the Malegam Committee to study the situation and make recommendations, based on which the first set of regulatory guidelines were issued.

These limits were revised further in April 2015, largely based on the recommendations of the Committee on Comprehensive Financial Services for Small Businesses and Low Income Households (Chairman: Dr Nachiket Mor). The limit on the total indebtedness of a borrower was raised to Rs 1,00,000 from Rs 50,000. The income criteria of borrowers for loans to be included as qualifying assets of these NBFCs changed – for borrowers with a rural household annual income not exceeding Rs 1,00,000 against Rs 60,000 earlier and urban and semi-urban household income not exceeding Rs 1,60,000 against Rs 1,20,000 earlier; ceiling on the amount of loan that could be disbursed was revised to Rs 60,000 from Rs 35,000 earlier in the first cycle and Rs 1,00,000 from Rs 50,000 earlier, in subsequent cycles. The income generating loan component was reduced from 70 per cent to 50 per cent. Further, now there is a mandatory repayment period of 24 months in the case of loans of Rs 30,000 and above. Guidelines on a fair practices code were also made applicable to these MFIs, which, inter alia, included a provision to display the effective annual interest rate charged by the MFI.

There has been criticism that the RBI should have regulated this sector much earlier so that the crisis in Andhra Pradesh could have been avoided. However, in the initial days, when microfinance was developing in the country, much hope was pinned on self-regulation by the sector. As experience showed, this did not happen. Subsequently, the RBI formally encouraged Self-Regulatory Organisations (SROs) to supplement the regulatory mechanism. There are two SROs, which have been recognised as such by the RBI, with SA-DHAN and MFIN, two microfinance providers' networks acting as SROs and taking care of certain regulatory requirements, such as enforcement of a code of conduct, operationalising a grievance redressal mechanism and submission of information to the Central Bank.

It is interesting to note that the microfinance sector in India during the period of development and consolidation, which was happening earlier, was sincerely hoping for some regulation to be in place and was actually looking forward to be regulated by the RBI, given the Central Bank's reputation in matters relating to regulation of banks and the fact that the RBI had been encouraging growth of this sector and the accompanying innovations and had been playing a proactive role in the development of the sector ever since its inception in the country. This is again a classic example of growth and innovation versus regulation that we have seen repeatedly in several contexts elsewhere in the world. The events finally overtook all intentions and NBFC-MFIs came to be regulated by the RBI. However, the question of regulating the other entities – the societies, trusts, and cooperatives, which were actively into microfinance, still remained. As discussed earlier, these institutions were set up under various central and state laws, but their Land microfinancing activities were not regulated under these laws. A separate legal and regulatory framework was necessary for these MFIs. To bridge this regulatory gap, the Government of India had introduced a bill in the Parliament in 2007, which could not be passed during the tenure of the Lok Sabha and lapsed[29]. It was again laid on the table when the next Lok Sabha was constituted. Even then it could not be seen through and lapsed once again. The Microfinance Development and Regulation Bill thus still lies in cold storage and unless a similar regulation comes into force, it will not be possible for MFIs to access deposits or thrifts, as it was named in the Bill, from the public and would continue to be deprived of low-cost funds. The very fact that MFIs are not in a position to access low-cost funds in the form of deposits or thrift pushes up their cost of funds and combined with their methods of operation, such as providing doorstep service to clients, makes their lending rates high as compared to banks, which can tap deposits at a relatively lower cost. A study by the College of Agricultural Banking, Pune in 2006 had shown that the interest rate to be charged by an MFI to break even was around 24 per cent per annum[30]. This was an average figure and there were wide variations on both sides. The MFIs that were able to lend at lower costs had access to low-cost funds from some source. It was also true that the MFIs, which charged considerably higher rates of interest on the loans, were at the end of the day responsible for the undesirable situation that the sector went into later, creating what was known as the crisis in Indian microfinance.

A significant regulatory requirement for NBFC-MFIs was that their lending rates should not exceed their cost of funds plus a margin of 10 per cent in the case of larger MFIs having an asset size over Rs 100 crore, and the cost of funds plus a margin of 12 per cent for other MFIs. Subsequently, as an alternative to this arrangement, MFIs were allowed to charge interest rates not exceeding 2.75 times the average base rates of five major commercial banks (by asset size).

There is another significant and fundamental issue associated with microfinance, basically with the group-based delivery model. The group model of microfinance delivery, which has been showing extremely good results in several parts of the country for several years, can at the most be a temporary arrangement. To start with, the group may comprise women from similar socio-economic background, but all members in the group do not possess the same capabilities. Although poor, some of them would show entrepreneurial traits, while some others would be satisfied with whatever little comes their way. It will be difficult for the first type to remain part of a group for long. Sooner or later, they would break away and form micro-enterprises of their own. The question is how to identify these members and how to provide them handholding support to help them graduate into micro-entrepreneurs. Additionally, members can always carry out a group-specific economic activity and, maybe, set up a micro-enterprise for the group as a whole. NABARD and SIDBI have been trying to facilitate this for quite some time but a general approach, which would hold good for the country, has not been found so far. The government as well as banks and financial institutions are committed to micro-enterprise development; but some acceptable way has to be found to help graduate SHGs or their members, who are capable, to a higher level, even if it means re-organising the group. There is also talk of 'Microfinance 3.0', or the third generation microfinance, in which, apart from sustainability, focus will be on responsible delivery and social outreach.

When financial inclusion was announced as an explicit policy focus in the middle of the last decade, one could assume that SHGs, with their experience of dealing with banks for both saving and credit, would provide an ideal route to effective financial inclusion. There was, however, a catch. In the SHG-Bank Linkage, the SHG was the 'person' who used to interact with the bank, had an account with it which was operated by designated members of the group, and all other members were beneficiaries of the process, without having bank accounts in their names and without in any way getting involved in financial transactions with the bank. Therefore, when the government decided to transfer the benefits given by it to its citizens by crediting to their bank accounts, whose account would it credit if the person was only a member of an SHG and did not have an independent bank account in her name? Thus, while for all other purposes the person may be considered as financially included, by virtue of not having an individual bank account, she would not qualify for being treated as fully financially included. Hence, in addition to the SHG having an account with some bank and the members already being aware of basic financial discipline, it became necessary for banks to open individual small accounts in the names of members.

The Cost of Lending

Any institution that provides some service incurs a cost and banks and MFIs are no exception. As we have seen, banks have set up a whole superstructure to take care of rural lending. They have the systems and processes and, of course, the people in place. All this involves expense. In the traditional public view, commercial banks are high-cost institutions. A paper, published by IFMR Finance Foundation in April 2013, showed that the total cost of rural credit delivery ranged from 13.75 per cent for a bank lending through an AA rated MFI, to 41.53 per cent for a public sector bank lending directly through its rural branches. The paper[31] concluded that the policy goals of achieving complete financial inclusion, building low-cost financial intermediation infrastructure and keeping the systemic risk low, would be best served by the use of well capitalised, high quality intermediaries instead of branches of banks, or even self-help groups.

Another study (Nathan Associates Inc., 2012)[32] concluded that public sector banks incurred a cost of 39.1 per cent on priority sector lending, as against a return of 11.5 per cent. Similar figures for private sector banks were 26.7 per cent and 14 per cent, respectively. This shows that the cost of lending to the priority sector by opening more branches is generally very high for all types of banks, whether in the public or private sector. Transaction cost depends on the number of transactions and number of accounts. Priority sector loans being small value loans spread over a large number of accounts, the transaction cost is high. This does not gel well with our notion that banks must lend directly to farmers or to other types of borrowers in the priority sector through their branches instead of lending indirectly through other organisations. Either we do not have faith in the capability of other intermediary organisations or we do not care for the profitability of banks. If providing a service entails such a high cost, appropriate ways must be found to earn revenues. Unless this happens, the banker's heart will not be there in these operations.

Obligation or Opportunity?

It is always interesting to reflect why commercial banks lend in the rural sector. Is it because of the policy that literally forces them to do so? Or do they see it as a social obligation? Or, maybe, it is considered a business opportunity, given the vast needs of finance in the rural economy and the fortune that lies at the so-called 'bottom of the pyramid'? A prudent reply would, of course, combine all three. The proportion may vary from person to person and would depend on the type of institution one is interacting with. For cooperative banks and later RRBs, LABs and later SFBs, rural finance has been an article of faith. They have been established for that purpose only. But for commercial banks, it all started with tremendous pressure from the government and the Central Bank to move to the rural sector and provide finance for various activities. It started with policy thrust and gradually people in the banking sector came to see it as a social obligation. They were moved by the situation around them, by the poverty and deprivation of the people and the exploitation by moneylenders. Many bankers have treated rural banking as service to the poor and have made tremendous impact in the area where they operated. Then a time came when our commercial banks, especially public sector banks, but also quite a few private sector banks, became familiar with rural finance. They had the necessary systems and processes in place to facilitate this and had several branches in the rural sector, which if not run profitably could be a heavy drain on their overall profitability and operational viability. Thus, many bankers came to treat rural finance as a profitable proposition. The quest for 'fortune at the bottom of the pyramid' and the way several other corporates handled the rural sector also made many bankers optimistic about the prospects of rural operations.

The explicit drive for financial inclusion in India, which started in the middle of the last decade, sought to leverage on the vast network of branches and their considerable experience in dealing with rural finance. Once again, the banking system was under pressure to go ahead and include those, not so far brought under the formal financial system. They were supposed to see the commercial angle in the whole exercise, to treat financial inclusion as a business opportunity. The exercise gave rise to much expectation among the public. As they say, the proof of the pudding lies in the eating. Policy may be fine, but sometimes it evaporates on reaching the ground. It is the practitioner's perception that matters. There seems to be neither an inherent demand among the socially and economically deprived classes, nor a profit-driving urge at the cutting-edge operating level of banks to wholeheartedly participate in the financial inclusion process.

Greater financial inclusion requires addressing constraints and taking advantage of opportunities in the financial ecosystem. Stakeholders are now beginning to focus on the diversity of clients on the basis of geography, income levels, livelihoods, gender, life cycle, etc., and their needs as well as the wide range of financial services (credit, savings, payments, insurance), financial service providers (MFIs, cooperatives, banks, insurance companies), and delivery channels (branches, BCs) to meet these needs. They are paying attention to the effectiveness of financial services as well as the knowledge and skills that clients need to use; the rules and regulations that guide financial markets; and the financial infrastructure such as payment systems and credit information bureaus required to support the system.

Micro-Insurance

Every serious illness, every accident and every natural disaster threatens the very existence of poor people and usually leads to deeper poverty. That's where micro-insurance comes in. Micro-insurance, the protection of low-income people against specific perils, in exchange for regular premium payments, proportionate to the likelihood and cost of the risk involved, seeks to provide a suitable solution for managing these risks. As per the Insurance Regulatory and Development Authority of India (IRDAI), the main thrust of micro-insurance regulations is to protect low-income people with affordable insurance products to help cope with and recover from common risks, with standardised popular insurance products, adhering to certain levels of cover, premium, and benefit standards. These regulations also allow both life and general insurers to promote 'combi-micro-insurance' products, which combine different types of insurance cover (life and non-life) in the same product[33].

A comparative evaluation of banking and non-banking financial products and services, needed and provided in our rural sector, shows that traditionally the thrust has been on provision of banking services, to the neglect of other types of financial services, particularly insurance. In fact, it can be argued that by being subject to the vagaries of weather and running several risks to life and health in the course of their occupations, the poor need insurance more than banking. At least the two should have gone hand-in-hand. Along with penetration of banking into the rural sector caused by several major policy initiatives of the Government, we should have also taken equally strong policy measures to spread insurance coverage in the rural sector. But for some inexplicable reason, this did not happen. That is why unlike banking, formal insurance sector's entry into rural areas has been rather slow.

This observation is also corroborated by the November 2017 report of the Household Finance Committee set up by the RBI (Chairman: Prof Tarun Ramadorai, Imperial College, London), which notes that the three main risks that households face, viz., loss of crops and livestock, major medical emergencies and damage to physical assets due to natural disasters, are all insurable. Wondering why households do not choose adequate insurance products to cover these risks, the Committee concludes that the most likely reasons are high transaction costs, lack of understanding of the details of the products and the distribution channel.

India is among the few countries to draft and implement specific micro-insurance regulations. In 2002, IRDA developed rural and social sector obligation norms that mandated every insurance company to achieve a certain percentage of polices to be sold in rural areas and the number of lives to be covered in the social sector. Once the IRDA regulations were put in place, it was the rural and social sector obligations that motivated insurance companies to venture into the rural sector and provide services to the financially excluded. The micro-insurance regulations promoted extensive use of intermediaries (micro-insurance agents) by the insurers for selling and servicing various micro-insurance products. The regulations clearly defined who could be the micro-insurance agents and allowed NGOs, community organisations and SHGs to act as agents. Such agents had to undergo compulsory training at the expense of the insurer. Later, in 2008, IRDA also allowed the then Section 25 companies (not-for-profit companies set up under Section 25 of the Companies Act, 1956) to act as micro-insurance agents. The regulations also attempted to manage the cost of intermediation by fixing commission caps for agents, which seemed to be more liberal than the normal commission rates to encourage participation.

In India, micro-insurance schemes have gathered momentum partly due to the development of microfinance activity and partly due to the regulation that makes it mandatory for all formal insurance companies to extend their activities to the rural and well-identified social sectors in the country. As a result, MFIs and NGOs are negotiating with the for-profit insurers for the purchase of customised group or standardised individual insurance schemes for the low-income people. Although the reach of such schemes is still very limited, they have considerable potential.

One of the greatest challenges for micro-insurance is the actual delivery to clients. Methods and models for doing so vary depending on the organisation, institution and provider involved. In general, there are four main methods for offering micro-insurance: the partner-agent model, the provider-driven model, the full-service model and the community-based model. Each of these models has its own advantages and disadvantages.

In a bid to boost the micro-insurance sector, IRDA has proposed to widen the product portfolio and distribution network of micro-insurance. It has proposed to allow cooperative banks, regional rural banks, primary agricultural co-operative societies and individuals such as shopkeepers, medical store owners, petrol pump owners and public telephone operators to act as micro-insurance agents. IRDA has noted that most of the products offered under this segment are basic ones and mostly term assurance; and has asked insurers to consider diversifying the micro-insurance portfolio by including saving-linked and health cover features. It has also said that the non-life retail insurance of the micro-insurance business might not be an attractive line of business at present, since it mainly covers individual risks such as dwelling, livestock and tools which are yet to be considered insurable by these segments. To cater to this segment, IRDA has proposed an option of appointing micro-insurance agents either to any one sector of micro enterprises, small enterprises and medium enterprises or to all three or any combination of two. Similarly, non-life insurers will also be allowed to appoint micro-insurance agents in these combinations either in the manufacturing sector or the service sector or in both.

Mis-selling of insurance products by insurance agents, both individual and institutions, has been a persistent problem faced by the sector. It has also been observed that in several cases, banks have sold insurance products at the time of issuing loans to unsuspecting borrowers, including even small borrowers. Spurious calls made in the names of IRDA, the RBI or government officials to members of the public for making investments or opening deposits, with the objective of having an insurance cover or otherwise, have also been a major issue. To tackle all this, financial literacy measures have been put in place by the regulator to make people aware of the requirements and to prevent them from falling prey to unscrupulous elements. Insurance intermediaries are also subject to a code of conduct as per IRDA regulations. The RBI also amended the Banking Ombudsman Scheme to include, inter alia, complaints against banks for mis-selling insurance products and to ensure suitability of the financial product being issued to a customer[34].

Pradhan Mantri Jan Dhan Yojana (PMJDY)

We have seen in the first chapter how the government's initiative to open bank accounts on a 'mission mode' yielded quick and effective results and how the banking sector ended up surpassing the target set by the government. When the PMJDY arrived on the scene in August 2014, financial inclusion was more than eight years old and in some sense banks were used to open 'no-frills accounts', subsequently named by the RBI as 'basic savings bank deposit accounts (BSBDA)'. SLBCs were entrusted with planning and monitoring of the financial inclusion exercise, first in districts with over 2000 population and then in the remaining districts with a bigger population. The BC system was getting somewhat stabilised after several experiments at the behest of the RBI and the government. In this backdrop, the PMJDY provided the much required focus and force to the government machinery to take financial inclusion to its logical conclusion. Once the accounts were in place, the government was quick to see further opportunities in this. An account holder could be provided insurance cover for life, as also some type of pension, by paying a small premium.

As on April 2018, the banking sector had opened more than 31 crore accounts, which had over Rs 79,000 crore in balance[35]. Remember that these accounts are supposed to be zero balance accounts. Seen by this yardstick, the programme has been eminently successful, at least in the first phase. The drive has been recognised even by the Guinness Book of World Records. In doing this, the banking sector in the country, comprising all types of banks, did feel the pressure and for quite some time initially, anecdotal evidence shows that the branches kept all other work aside to complete this task. But at the end of the day, the level of linkage with banks that was achieved was revolutionary by any account. Now that the accounts were opened, they had to be operated and banks were asked to allow a small overdraft of Rs 5,000 in these accounts after six months. Some banks did provide such an overdraft in a graded manner, starting with Rs 500 or Rs 1,000 and slowly going up, while some others allowed the entire Rs 5,000. Through financial literacy initiatives, taken up by banks, the government as also private agencies and individuals, account holders were exhorted to put small deposits in these accounts. The government too promised to channelise benefits including subsidies through these accounts so that the account holder had enough incentive to continue holding the account and not letting it become inoperative after some time. However, in spite of all this, ensuring transactions in these accounts has been a huge challenge.

The PMJDY account came with a RuPay debit card, provided by the National Payments Corporation of India (NPCI). The card came bundled with a life insurance cover of Rs 30,000 subject to certain conditions. To be eligible for coverage, the card was required to be operated at least once every 45 days. Subsequently, under the Pradhan Mantri Jeevan Jyoti Bima Yojana (PMJJBY), a life cover of Rs 2 lakh was made available to the PMJDY account holders in the age group of 18 to 50 years at a premium of Rs 330 per annum per member. The insurance cover is renewed every year. Accident insurance cover was made available to them through the Pradhan Mantri Suraksha Bima Yojana (PMSBY), under which a cover of Rs 2 lakh was provided for accidental death and permanent total disability and Rs 1 lakh for permanent partial disability. Account holders in the age group of 18 to 70 years were made eligible for coverage with a premium of Rs 12 per annum, and the policy was subject to renewal every year.

The holders of PMJDY accounts were also brought under a pension scheme, named Atal Pension Yojana (APY), under which, a guaranteed monthly pension of Rs 1,000 to Rs 5,000 was payable per month to the pensioners on attaining the age of 60 years, depending on their contribution and based on the age of joining the scheme. The minimum age of joining the APY was fixed at 18 years and the maximum age at 39 years, which left the minimum period of contribution by any subscriber under the APY at 20 years. The total contribution would be Rs 1,000 per annum and the Central Government would contribute 50 per cent of the amount. The focus of the scheme was on citizens in the unorganised sector.

While insurance schemes are being operated by the Life Insurance Corporation of India, the pension scheme is being operationalised by the Pension Fund Regulatory and Development Authority (PFRDA). The financial inclusion drive in the country was aimed at providing not only banking services but also insurance and pension services in the rural and disadvantaged sectors. In the case of the PMJDY, one can see comprehensive financial inclusion in action.

3

The Demand Factor – Facilitating the First Mile Walk

IN the quest for financial inclusion of the excluded people in the rural sector, the government has been historically occupied with the supply side push through conscious policy focus. Whenever necessary, the government has applied force on the players to behave and also allow new players to come in and compete in the field. The generally accepted logic seems to be that once the infrastructure is in place, people would start using it sooner or later. Once the branch of a bank is established in a village, the villagers would gradually start availing the banking facility and the branch would at some point in time also reach out to the potential customers, at least in its own interest, if not for anything else.

However, supply has not always created its own demand. In a country where we still talk about the low level of general literacy in many regions, lack of financial literacy or lack of basic knowledge of financial matters can deter people from dealing with formal institutions. It can be fear of possible rejection by the bank branch, not being comfortable with the ambience or environment, which may look unfriendly, or some other real or perceived disadvantage. Mere opening of a bank branch would not ensure banking for all, as mere opening of bank accounts would not lead to financial inclusion. We can make financial services available and affordable for the people but the actual usage would depend to a great extent on the ground-level realities, the economic potential of the area, awareness of the people as to why they should deal with banks and in what manner it would fit in their lives and take care of their needs.

For service providers, it is eminently necessary to know what their existing as well as prospective customers want and accordingly customise their products and services to be delivered to them. Although broadly speaking, this is also applicable to banks, they usually have standardised products for the clients of small means and generally customisation in this segment is rare. First, it is not cost-effective to provide small-value services to a large number of clients whose income and cash flow are highly irregular and who do not own any appreciable assets. Second, the staff working in the branches may not be fully familiar or comfortable with the local economy and the people. Traditionally, loans have been of certain fixed types and deposits are as per the policies of the bank, applicable to all depositors. It is generally difficult to customise these things for rural customers. This has also been one of the reasons for exclusion of the rural poor from the formal banking system. There was hardly any suitable product to match the irregular cash flow and income pattern, as also the small amounts of disposable income or saving of the prospective customer. Even RRBs, which were set up to mainly take care of the financial needs of the rural sector, have been no different from commercial banks.

One answer to this lack of customisation was microfinance. The microfinance sector flourished because of their close understanding of the client needs and their income pattern. Whether it was microfinance provided by the not-for-profit organisations or by the for-profit MFIs, tailor-made products to suit the local clientele was what these organisations specialised in. In the initial days of microfinance, several well-meaning institutions were active in this area and were often seen working in difficult situations alongside their clients. Starting with Grameen Bank of Bangladesh and many others, banks, NGOs and MFIs who came subsequently, based on different models of delivery, microfinance was seen as a highly workable mechanism for providing flexible financial services to the poor to suit their needs.

In India, the Self Help Group (SHG)-Bank Linkage Programme, which was started in 1992 by NABARD, sought to address the issue from the viewpoint of the banking sector. This was a model where microfinance was sought to be provided by banks, not directly to a person but to a group of persons, established on the ground of commonality of interest and working on the strength of group dynamics. While banks lacked flexibility in service delivery, the deficiency was made good by operating in groups. A group would take over part of the credit cycle and initially make saving habit more important than taking a loan. The target group for SHGs was mostly women, as elsewhere, since women in low income and economically disadvantaged households were seen as better managers of their meagre financial resources, and hence more dependable in financial matters. Such loans, taken for a variety of purposes, were generally repaid to the groups and then to banks as per the schedule and default was negligible. The superstructure of microfinance in India was actually based on these simple but effective principles. Here was a system which seemed to address all the weaknesses of the formal financial system in matters relating to financing the poor.

Microfinance, we have discussed in the previous chapter, has passed through several stages and almost all countries, where micro-finance operated in some form, experienced turbulence later at some point. Problems arose because the system was commercialised to a great extent, too much expansion was happening too fast, without taking care of actual customer needs, lack of patience in waiting for concrete results, diluting systems and processes, checks and balances as institutions progressed and grew larger, and adopting questionable methods in extending and collection of loans. Financial access to the poor, which came at a heavy cost to them, was in many cases a road to making abnormal profits and the whole superstructure at some point of time seemed to be resting on soft clay. A wonderful innovation, which would have helped the system to address all the financial needs of the excluded persons, turned out to be saddled with the same problems that were common in mainstream banking and finance, including the problem of loan delinquency.

As so brilliantly presented in the book 'Portfolios of the Poor' by Daryl Collins, Jonathan Morduch, Orlanda Ruthven and Stuart Rutherford[1], the poor with small means are good financial planners. They do not have any formal training, nor are they aware of any systems and processes. They do their planning in almost an involuntary manner. Because their resources are extremely limited, they need to do a lot of planning so as to allocate the meagre resources properly. There is a need for education and awareness building here so that they learn to plan methodically, to distinguish between good and bad ways of allocating resources, and to avoid the common pitfalls that people without any financial education regularly face in our country.

It is very common to find people being cheated by unscrupulous elements, whether individuals or companies and other entities, and falling prey to their machinations and parting with their hard-earned savings. The matter is complicated further by the absence of formal financial institutions in several areas of the country; and wherever they are present, there is deep fear and mistrust towards them. Such exploitations by fly-by-night operators have in fact been quite common and from time to time, one hears how people lost their entire savings in the process. This calls for urgent measures to provide financial education to all, especially to the vulnerable people, many of whom also lack normal literacy. The financial sector regulators, both the RBI and IRDA, regularly run advertisements and have displays on their websites urging people not to fall prey to such promises for high returns and to verify the bona fides of such entities before entrusting them with their hard-earned savings. They need to understand clearly that there is nothing like a free lunch and that more perceived return in the financial sector comes with more risk, often the risk of losing the entire amount invested.

Rural people do have needs for financial services but these have to be converted to effective demand for them. This would be their first step towards financial institutions and towards financial inclusion. Awareness and literacy are absolutely essential for people to take that step. Financial literacy is the most important pre-requisite for meaningful financial inclusion. There are barriers which people have to overcome and it is not always easy. On their part, financial institutions must re-orient their processes and tune them to the needs of people. To quote Vijay Mahajan, a doyen of Indian microfinance industry, "The young person who begins work after education can be offered a number of financial services, from a simple bank account, enabling receiving and making payments, to term-deposits, to medium-term savings for buying a home, if necessary supplemented with a housing loan; health insurance and life insurance; and long-term savings for pension after retirement. Finally, in many cultures, getting a dignified burial or cremation and a death ceremony after that is important and a savings product could be designed for that. The life cycle approach is completely absent in our financial thinking, financial offering and financial regulation"[2].

Apart from literacy and awareness, people's behaviour also determines their choice of financial product and service. Understanding how consumers' behaviour translates into financial service needs, requires understanding the uniqueness and heterogeneity of clients and how life cycle events, livelihoods, geography, income levels and gender and several other cultural factors influence their behaviour. Our financial institutions are generally not in a position to study such behaviour and understand its implications and effects, maybe because they do not have sufficient people who can study this on an ongoing basis and provide inputs for operational efficiency and also because the people who man these organisations do not have the time required for such an endeavour. Of course, as always, there are exceptions and wherever this happens, organisations become successful and contribute positively to the development process.

Banking is fundamentally a commercial activity, as banks accept deposits and make loans and investments, in the process earning a profit that keeps them alive. In order that potential clients, big or small, understand the products and services that they put on offer, banks must explain them to the clients. As some people say, customers, who are more aware and literate, are better customers, notwithstanding the fact that they also can be more difficult customers.

Financial Literacy

For a person who has never used the banking system for any purpose, taking the first mile walk into the system needs a lot of awareness as to why she should deal with banks and in what manner it would help her in her day-to-day life. With small and irregular cash flows and their consequent impact on a person's ability to perform certain essential tasks in life, dealing with banks does not always seem a necessary option to these people. Conventional banks are generally seen as institutions built to support the financially well off and those having regular income streams, not those who have been described by some as 'financial nomads', not having regular income or assets[3]. If at all, we want them to interact with banks, financial literacy needs to be properly designed to induce them to take that voluntary step towards the banking system.

According to its literal definition, financial literacy is the ability to use skills and knowledge to take effective and informed money-management decisions. For a country like India, this plays a bigger role as it is considered an important adjunct to promotion of financial inclusion and ultimately financial stability.

As per a global survey by American financial services company, Standard & Poor's Financial Services, less than 25 per cent of adults are financially literate in South Asian countries. For an average Indian, financial literacy is yet to become a priority. India is home to 17.5 per cent of the world's population but nearly 76 per cent of its adult population does not understand even the basic financial concepts[4]. The survey confirms that financial literacy in India has consistently been poor compared to the rest of the world. Financial illiteracy puts a burden on the nation in the form of higher cost of financial security and lesser prosperity. An example of this is the fact that most people resort to investing more in physical assets and short-term instruments, which conflicts with the greater need for long-term investments, both for households to meet their life-stage goals and for meeting the country's capital requirements for infrastructure.

In India, there are also certain erroneous beliefs associated with financial literacy, the most common being the myth that one who is 'educated' or 'rich' is also 'financially literate'. In reality, it may not be so. The financial system is anything but simple. Financial literacy operates at different levels and a person can be literate in some aspects of finance but illiterate in some other aspects. Lack of basic financial understanding leads to unproductive investment decisions. The financial world is ever changing and its complexity ever increasing. In such a scenario, it is difficult for even an educated person to keep track of all the developments and changes and taking appropriate financial decisions. So is the case with the not so educated and the uneducated who form a sizeable part of the population. Along with relative financial illiteracy, we also have to fight absolute financial illiteracy.

Another myth is that financial literacy is more important for adults. We can achieve the desired results from financial literacy only when we start educating our children. Like many other provocative topics, money is something that children hear about outside homes as well, which exposes them to wrong perceptions, unless they are consciously told about the characteristics of money.

Financial regulators in India – the RBI, the Securities and Exchange Board of India (SEBI), IRDA and the Pension Fund Regulatory and Development Authority (PFRDA) have created a joint charter called 'National Strategy for Financial Education', detailing initiatives taken by them and also other market participants like banks, stock exchanges, broking houses, mutual funds and insurers. Simultaneously, all regulators as also all service providers are to various degrees engaged in spreading financial literacy. As per the RBI guidelines issued in 2009, banks were required to open Financial Literacy and Credit Counselling Centres (FLCCs) at district headquarters and in other places. Subsequently, these were renamed Financial Literacy Centres (FLCs). Banks have, as a result, opened FLCs at the district and *taluka* or block levels. At present, there are about 1300 FLCs operated by banks in the country. These are manned by serving or retired bankers. The effectiveness of an FLC often depends on the zeal and dedication of the person-in-charge rather than any structural or institutional factor. While some of them have made good progress in reaching out to people and spreading financial literacy in their areas of operation, many others have just managed to move along. On the whole, it seems the FLC system is under-utilised. To make FLCs robust, banks need to give appropriate compensation to the persons looking after the centres and for that they need to see that FLCs are centres that would contribute to their profitability in the long run by getting more clients and also more informed clients.

Financial inclusion and education are two important elements in the RBI's developmental role. Towards this, it has created a large volume of literature that has been uploaded on its website in 13 languages for banks and other stakeholders to download and use. The aim of this initiative is to create awareness about financial products and services, good financial practices, going digital and consumer protection. The RBI has also asked banks to conduct financial literacy camps in villages through its branches serving these areas. Since its Diamond Jubilee year (2009), the RBI and thereafter several other banks started conducting outreach visits to remote places with the objective of spreading financial literacy and also understanding the realities in the countryside. This was driven by the then RBI Governor, Dr Duvvuri Subbarao, who while assuming Governorship had resolved to 'keep his ears to the ground' and to help the RBI understand that behind every policy action, there are 'people', whose interests have to be kept in mind[5]. The top brass of the bank started visiting villages under the Outreach Programmes and interacted with the common man. This was something unprecedented for a Central Bank anywhere in the world. Simultaneously, officers of the bank also interacted with school and college students and interacted with the public in regularly held 'town hall' events.

Banks have been exploring all possible ways to spread financial literacy. Along with FLCs, several banks also established stalls in various exhibitions all over the country. This move was also spearheaded by the RBI, which even today opens stalls in almost all well-known exhibitions and trade fairs, not only in state capitals but at times also in district headquarters and other small towns. This provided banks an opportunity not only to spread financial literacy by interacting with the visitors but also to promote usage of their own products and services among potential customers. The government and local administration have also partnered with banks and other organisers to facilitate the process. Another interesting way to promote financial literacy, which was started by the NABARD and the RBI, involved writing of messages on trains and buses. These were usually in the local language and were accompanied by pictorial representations of simple concepts in banking, which urged the travellers not to fall prey to the machinations of unscrupulous elements while investing their hard-earned money.

Several NGOs and corporates and other private sector organisations have carried forward these initiatives and started conducting not only regular classes and interactive sessions but also seminars and conferences on the theme of financial literacy and inclusion. They have moved to schools and colleges as also other institutions and tried to impart financial knowledge in some form to the students and other participants of these programmes. Pamphlets, handbills, stickers, bags, caps, etc. have been used to carry messages on financial matters. Advertisements on the radio and television as also in cinema halls have also been used. In this regard, it is important to note that empirical evidence points to the fact that digital efforts like video clips, short films and interactive quizzes on financial education have had a far greater impact than the traditional medium.

In some states, the RBI has coordinated with the state governments to include financial literacy material in the school curriculum. The initiative started in Karnataka and the next state to adopt this was Andhra Pradesh, then undivided. In the latter, topics on banking and financial matters, including currency notes, were first included in the Social Studies syllabus for Class IX and then for Class X. After the division of the state, both Andhra Pradesh and Telangana have continued the measure, with appropriate revision whenever necessary. This has been a major initiative so far as financial literacy is concerned, as school children are the best target group for inculcating financial awareness. If they are aware in such matters, they would be better citizens of the future. Through them, their parents and others with whom they interact would also become aware and in cases where they are already aware, their memory would be refreshed.

Additionally, the RBI also launched a financial literacy drive in 80 blocks in nine states on a pilot basis to educate people, inter alia, on e-transactions, borrowing from financial institutions and insurance purchases. Termed as the Centre for Financial Literacy

(CFL) project, it is executed through six NGOs registered with the Depositor Education and Awareness Fund (DEAF), in collaboration with banks.

As per the National Strategy for Financial Education (NSFE), the key components of financial education efforts could include understanding the key financial products one may need throughout one's life, including bank accounts, insurance, retirement savings plans and securities market investments like stocks, bonds and mutual funds; understanding basic financial concepts like compound interest, present and future value of money, annuity, investment return, risk, protection and diversification, and so on; developing skills and confidence to be aware of financial risk and opportunities and to benefit from them; and making good financial choices about saving, spending, insurance, investing and managing debt throughout one's life: for example, when getting an education, starting a job, buying a house, starting a family, getting ready to retire and living out the senior years.

The NSFE's mission speaks about undertaking a massive financial education campaign to help people manage money more effectively to achieve financial well-being. This is done by accessing appropriate financial products and services through regulated entities with fair and transparent machinery for consumer protection and grievance redressal and conducting financial education campaigns across the country for all sections of the population along with awareness campaigns at different levels for existing and potential customers to improve the knowledge, understanding, skills and competence in managing money effectively to improve their financial status by taking an informed decision. The mission would be accomplished through provision of financial education throughout the life cycle of an individual starting from the school level. The endeavour is to ensure the well-being of individuals through financial inclusion.

As per the RBI guidelines, financial education is also required to be customised to meet the requirements of different target groups, in addition to the basic financial literacy that every person is expected to have. Financial literacy is important for several occupation groups, such as farmers, micro-entrepreneurs, traders, etc. During the conduct of their day-to-day activities and interaction with banks for various purposes, these people are exposed to financial decision-making, with various levels of complexity. A farmer must understand the basics of crop finance as also finance for development of land, purchase of bullock or setting up a small poultry farm, along with details of where finance is available and on what terms, and when and how crop insurance would be helpful. The micro entrepreneur must also be familiar with the avenues of financial assistance available to him, including bank finance for various schemes. The Micro and Small Enterprise (MSME) sector in the country, in which the extent of financial exclusion is very high, stands to benefit much from the spread of literacy. It is shocking to see that in the MSME sector, only 5.3 per cent obtain finance from institutional sources, mainly banks[6]. The remaining overwhelming majority, which either takes financial assistance from non-institutional sources (about 2 per cent) or from elsewhere or uses own funds, constitute a vast segment of the micro and small entrepreneur class. They are in acute need of awareness in financial matters relating to operation of their enterprises. In the absence of these guidelines, not only are they misguided by others but they are also not able to function optimally. Money is the life blood of any enterprise and it must be managed appropriately for the enterprise to survive, progress and expand.

In our country, the focus in rural banking had traditionally been on lending. Targets are set for lending in the form of Priority Sector Lending (PSL) by commercial banks as also through various other schemes and programmes of the government. There are forums set up under the Lead Bank Scheme, which plan and monitor the lending process and follow up with individual banks. Giving a loan is only half of the credit cycle. The remaining half, comprising loan utilisation and collection, is also equally important. While all the forums monitor lending, there is no centralised way of monitoring loan utilisation and recovery. Each lender is supposed to do it in her own interest. However, this does not always happen. In the decibel of lending, for which the government itself puts enormous pressure on banks, the borrower forgets that what she is getting is a 'loan' which has to be repaid in time with interest. This, coupled with the loan waivers described earlier in this book, quite often lead the borrower to believe that these loans need not be repaid at all. As a result, the banking sector suffers. The credit cycle gets choked. Although it is not easy to find a solution to this problem, the only effective way seems to be through proper education and awareness building as also through development of robust safety nets. The banking sector must speak in one voice and go on continuously educating the public on the need for loan repayment, which will happen if the loan is used for the purpose for which it is taken, other things remaining constant.

We have seen how a large number of organisations and individuals are engaged in spreading financial literacy in the country. In some areas, the activities of different organisations seem to overlap. What is required is a joint effort by all the banking, financial services and insurance companies as well, to be able to achieve noticeable changes in the perceptions that an average Indian has about financial management. It is time to bring individual efforts under one framework to ensure better outcomes. The efforts at the level of banks may continue to be coordinated by the State Level Bankers' Committee (SLBC) but another dedicated institution would perhaps be in a better position to plan, implement, monitor and evaluate financial literacy measures on a wider canvas.

Financial literacy assumes greater significance in the context of digital transactions, which will be covered in detail in the next chapter. Digital transactions call for some basic knowledge of electronic methods in addition to the underlying financial process. This involves a third tier of literacy after normal literacy and basic financial literacy. A person, who owns or has been issued a debit card or a credit card, must know how to use it, how best to use it so that she gets all benefits associated with it and how to avoid its misuse. Nowhere has this assumed more urgency than in the case of the PMJDY, where the first-time entrants into the banking system through a 'basic banking account' or a 'small account' have also to learn how to use a RuPay Card and what happens if the card is not used for a considerable period of time. The accident insurance cover associated with the RuPay Card remains valid only if the card is used at least once in 45 days, which many card holders are not aware of.

The same agencies which are active in promoting financial literacy are also engaged in improving digital financial literacy. The field is vast and the gap is too wide for any single agency to be able to cover. There is also a need to continuously update and engage in providing repeated doses. Financial literacy is a process, not an event.

The Cost of Literacy

One final point about financial literacy. In a bank-dominated economy, banks are ultimately expected to promote financial literacy, either on their own or in association with other agencies, including government and non-governmental organisations. This, it can be argued, is in a bank's own interest, as otherwise it would not be getting informed customers who would understand and appreciate its products and services on offer. However, conducting of camps, setting up FLCs, participating in exhibitions, etc., all involve cost. There are also indirect costs in the form of lost time and forgone work in branches when the staff goes out for financial literacy camps. Ideally, the cost should be borne by the service providers, banks themselves, as in the process of spreading financial literacy banks are also making people aware of their products and services. But in a scenario where banks are struggling for profit and have to frequently go for branch rationalisation and reduction in the number of fresh recruits, incurring a cost to further financial literacy becomes an issue. This is a much bigger issue for RRBs and cooperative banks in view of their generally low profitability.

A Financial Inclusion Fund (FIF) has been established with NABARD with a corpus of Rs 2,000 crore with a view to, inter alia, capacity building and creation of awareness to address demand side issues. Eligible activities for funding under the FIF include setting up of financial inclusion and literacy centres up to the block level, providing financial literacy training to all individuals and households in the area, counselling services for opening of bank accounts and also the training of BCs. Financial assistance is given to banks and financial institutions, who can also work with NGOs, SHGs, Farmers' Clubs, functional cooperatives, PACS, IT-enabled rural outlets of corporate entities, well-functioning *panchayat*s and Common Service Centres (CSCs) set up under the National e-Governance Plan.

At the end of the financial year 2016-17, the cumulative sanctions under the FIF stood at Rs 2,687 crore, with disbursements of Rs 1,301 crore. Assistance for spreading financial literacy is also provided out of the Depositor Education and Awareness Fund (DEAF), maintained with the RBI, to NGOs on a selective basis[6].

Financial literacy can be seen as a 'public good', as absence of it can lead to disastrous consequences, often at high cost to the system. If some bank consciously decides to bear all expenses in connection with financial literacy measures, it should be fine. Such a bank would see financial literacy expenses as an investment that would in due course pay dividends to the bank in the form of increased clientele and better customer interface. Otherwise, the coordinating agency for financial education, when set up by the government, can perhaps take over the responsibility to offer financial assistance to various players for taking steps to promote financial literacy. Till then, at least a part of the expenses that banks incur in their continuing efforts to spread financial literacy can be reimbursed to them by the government, or by the Central Bank, in the interest of the public. In any enterprise, money matters must be cleared upfront, lest it result in a half-hearted approach.

Skill Development

Demand for banking services is closely related to the occupation of a person. A farmer or a micro entrepreneur would have her specific requirement of financial assistance, which would depend on farming or industrial activity or trade undertaken by her. It is evident that if people are trained for undertaking some livelihood development activities, their standard of living as well as their need for credit and other banking facilities would improve. Providing livelihood to the young in this country has been one of the major tasks of any government. Unless the youth get opportunities for employment or some vocation, the demographic dividend would elude the country and become a demographic disaster. As the saying goes, give a man a fish, and you feed him for a day; teach him fishing, and you feed him for a lifetime.

While there are several initiatives in the country aimed at skilling of the rural youth, our banking system has been associated with the process for above two decades. In 1982, Canara Bank and Syndicate Bank, in association with the Shree Dharmasthala Manjunatheswara Education Trust in Karnataka, set up Rural Development and Self Employment Training Institutes (RUDSETIs) to train rural youth for making them capable of undertaking self-employment ventures. Subsequently, 27 RUDSETIs were set up in different states all over the country. The initiative was inspired by Dr D. Veerandra Heggade, Chairman of the Dharmasthala Foundation, who said, "Instead of writing someone else's account through wage employment after three to five years of collegiate education, it is more meaningful to write one's own account by embarking upon some self-employment"[7].

Inspired by the success of the RUDSETI model, the Government of India, Ministry of Rural Development decided in 2009 to establish Rural Self-Employment Training Institutes (RSETIs) in the country and provide funding and other support for the same. Lead Banks in districts were assigned the responsibility to open RSETIs in their districts, with necessary support also from state governments and the banks themselves. As on date, 586 RSETIs have been established by banks all over the country, with the objective of imparting good quality training to the rural youth in various vocations. As on November 2017, RSETIs had trained cumulatively more than 25 lakh youth, with the settlement percentage at 66. However, 45 per cent of self-employed persons had received credit linkage from banks.

In establishing RSETIs, the government clearly had in mind the need for credit linkage at a later stage and setting up these institutes through banks was itself a measure aimed at ensuring this. These institutes have been set up with a lot of expectations, apart from resources spent to create the infrastructure. Hence, there must be a long-term vision for RSETIs. At this stage itself, RSETIs have been burdened with the issues of getting participants regularly for training programmes, finding faculty members who can handle training sessions, following up after training to facilitate credit linkage and, of course, ensuring that a good percentage of trainees actually get settled, preferably with self-employment ventures. It is true that the Government of India is encouraging skill development like never before but in the process, several other initiatives have been taken and the RSETI network finds itself without a long-term action plan.

Deposit Insurance

The confidence of the public in the banking system is essentially what keeps the system functional. Typically, a person does not verify a bank's soundness before opening an account and depositing her hard-earned money there. She is confident that the money would be safe in the bank's vaults and in the unlikely case of the bank failing, the government and the RBI would take care of her money. This may not be entirely true, for deposit insurance law in our country does not provide for cover to the entire deposits but only one lakh rupees of deposits in any account is protected by the Deposit Insurance and Credit Guarantee Corporation (DICGC), which is a subsidiary of the RBI. There have been talks of increasing this amount but it has not happened. Instead, another institution, the Financial Resolution and Deposit Insurance Corporation (FRDIC), is proposed to be established to take care of bank failures as well as deposit insurance[8]. The FRDIC Bill is being discussed in the public domain and a clear picture is yet to emerge. There are gaps in the bill relating to deposit insurance which hopefully would be addressed by the time it becomes law. Be that as it may, banking hinges on trust. The common man puts his money in a bank because of the trust that he has and it is the duty of the government to protect that trust, particularly when it is forcing citizens to open bank accounts to help electronic transfer of benefits resulting in financial inclusion. In the present scenario, the insurance cover of Rs 1 lakh comes with a premium, which is paid by the bank and is not charged to the depositor. In several countries, the government does provide such deposit insurance, the most well-known being the Federal Deposit Insurance Corporation (FDIC) of the USA, which protects deposits of up to USD 2500. In the financial crisis of 2008, the FDIC worked alongside the Federal Government and the Federal Reserve to ensure that the financial institutions affected by the crisis did not fail.

In India, the only beneficiaries of deposit insurance so far have been depositors of small urban cooperative banks. These banks, as we have seen before, are established mostly on community basis and through individual initiatives. Being generally small, these banks are subject to failure at even relatively minor shocks; their systems are not robust and they fail to employ good people who can understand and deliver appropriate service. Once such a bank fails to meet the standards set by the regulator, a series of actions follow, which may sometimes lead to the licence of the bank getting cancelled, in which case, it ceases to operate. The Registrar of Cooperative Societies of the state government is then approached to complete the process of liquidation of the bank. Once this situation develops, the DICGC sets in motion a process of payment of insured deposits, first to small depositors and then to others. Although commercial banks and regional rural banks also pay the insurance premium, there has been no instance where the DICGC has been called upon to pay their depositors.

Consumer Protection

Expansion of the reach of banking and financial services and addition of more and more consumers to the list of exiting users of these services is closely related to the issue of consumer protection. In India, the quality of service extended by banks has often been poor in spite of measures put in place by the regulator from time to time.

Protection of the interests of depositors has been one of the mandates of the RBI. The Banking Regulation Act, 1949 is replete with phrases like "in the interest of depositors" wherever it entrusts powers to the RBI be it granting of a banking licence or cancellation thereof, giving directions on advances or on any banking matter, applying for suspension, winding up, or amalgamation of banks, approving appointment of CEOs or additional directors, removal of CEOs, all these are to be exercised keeping, among other things, and the depositors' interests in view. But the services provided by the banking sector today are much more than only deposit services. This rapid increase in the nature of financial services has highlighted the need for robust regulation as well as consumer education to protect and empower consumers. The need to extend provision of banking services to underserved sections of the population whose financial literacy is low, combined with the growing complexity of financial products and the use of technology, can increase the risk of mis-selling. If such protection is absent, the benefits to economic growth of expanded financial inclusion may be severely undermined. Financial consumer protection also contributes to strengthening financial stability.

Apart from the RBI, the Government of India has also been concerned with financial consumer protection. The Financial Sector Legislative Reforms Commission (FSLRC) was constituted by the Ministry of Finance in March 2011 and was asked to comprehensively review and redraw the legislations governing India's financial system. In its report submitted to the Ministry of Finance in March 2013, containing a draft Indian Financial Code to replace the bulk of the existing financial laws, the Commission has amply highlighted the issue of consumer protection.

The work of the Commission in the field of consumer protection marks a watershed compared with traditional approaches in Indian financial law. It marks a break with the tradition of caveat emptor, the 'buyers beware' concept and moves towards a position where a significant burden of consumer protection is placed upon financial firms. The draft Financial Code first establishes certain basic rights for all financial consumers and then defines what is an unsophisticated consumer and an additional set of protections are defined for these consumers. As per the proposed basic protections, financial service providers must act with professional diligence and the system must provide protection against unfair contract terms, protection against unfair conduct, protection of personal information and redress of complaints by financial service providers. In addition, unsophisticated consumers will have three additional protections: (i) the right to receive suitable advice; (ii) protection from conflicts of interest of advisors; and access to the redress agency for redress of grievances.

Most important, perhaps, was the release of the Charter of Consumer Rights by the RBI in December 2014, which enshrined broad, overarching principles for the protection of bank customers and enunciates the 'five' basic rights of bank customers[13]. These are: (i) Right to fair treatment, (ii) Right to transparency, fair and honest dealing, (iii) Right to suitability, (iv) Right to privacy, and (v) Right to grievance redress and compensation. The RBI also advised the Indian Banks' Association (IBA) and the Banking Codes and Standards Board of India (BCSBI) to formulate a "Model Customer Rights Policy" encapsulating the principles enshrined in the Charter. All the scheduled commercial banks, regional rural banks and urban cooperative banks have accordingly prepared their own board-approved policy incorporating the five basic rights of the Charter, which also contains a monitoring and oversight mechanism for ensuring adherence.

Know Your Customer (KYC) guidelines is another area where the experience of bank customers has not been very good. Initiated by the government with the objective of ensuring that only genuine persons availed of banking services and that the banking system was, knowingly or unknowingly, not used for money laundering by unscrupulous elements, KYC norms have often proved to be irritants in banker-customer relationship. While no one would argue against a mechanism to screen customers for ensuring safe and sound banking, it was people with small means who suffered the most, as it was difficult for them to arrange all the required documents to prove their genuineness at the time of opening a bank account. Some exception, therefore, had to be made to facilitate financial inclusion.

The RBI undertook several measures to educate consumers on KYC norms, including releasing a note along with a poster and a booklet comprising a few common questions relating to KYC norms for opening bank accounts. The objective was to bring awareness among the general public about the KYC simplification measures taken by the RBI in the recent times with a view to helping the common man in opening bank accounts.

The measures taken for simplification of KYC include prescribing a single document for proof of identity and proof of address, removing the requirement for separate proof of address for current address, making KYC a bank process rather than a branch process, relaxing the officially valid documents (OVDs) for low-risk customers, increasing the time intervals for periodic updation of KYC for existing low-, medium- and high-risk customers from five years, two years, and one year, to 10, eight, and two years, respectively. Banks are not expected to seek fresh proofs of identity and address at the time of periodic updation from those customers who are categorised as 'low risk', in case of no change in status with respect to their identities and addresses. A self-certification by the customer to that effect should suffice in such cases and banks may not insist on physical presence of such low-risk customer at the time of periodic updation. Further, if an existing KYC-compliant customer of a bank desires to open another account in the same bank, there should be no need for submission of fresh proof of identity and proof of address for the purpose. Business Correspondents and Business Facilitators were allowed to act as Customer Service Point (CSP) for e-KYC purpose. A highly simplified KYC requirement was put in place in the case of 'small accounts' as defined under the Prevention of Money Laundering Act (PMLA), 2002, which defines a small account as one in which the balance does not exceed Rs 50,000, total credits do not exceed Rs 1 lakh during a year, and withdrawals during a month do not exceed Rs 10,000. For opening such accounts, a simple declaration is enough. However, the validity of this process is for one year and the account holder has to submit one of the required documents within that period.

To enhance transparency in fixing of interest rates on loans, the RBI has advised banks to display on their website, inter alia, the interest rate range of contracted loans for the past quarter for different categories of advances granted to individual borrowers, along with mean interest rates for such loans, the total fees and charges applicable on various types of loans to an individual borrower, which should also be disclosed at the time of processing of loan for transparency and comparability and to facilitate informed decision making by customers; Annual Percentage Rate (APR) or such similar other arrangement of representing the total cost of credit on a loan to an individual borrower so as to allow customers to compare the costs associated with borrowing across products and lenders. Apart from displaying such information, banks are also required to provide a clear, concise, one-page fact-sheet to all individual borrowers at every stage of loan processing as well as in case of any change in any terms and conditions.

While undertaking insurance distribution business, either under the corporate agency or broking model under the relevant IRDA regulations, banks were directed to put in place a system of assessment of the suitability of products for customers and classify products into universally suitable products and complex products, which necessarily require a customer's assessment prior to sale. It should be ensured that there is a standardised system of assessing the needs of the customer and that initiation, transactional and approval processes are segregated. Banks should treat their customers fairly, honestly and transparently with regard to suitability and appropriateness of the insurance product sold. They should not follow any restrictive practice of forcing a customer to either opt for products of a specific insurance company or link sale of such products to any banking product. It should be prominently stated in all publicity material distributed by a bank that the purchase by the bank's customer of any insurance products is purely voluntary and is not linked to availing of any other facility from the bank. Further, the details of fees or brokerage received in respect of insurance broking or agency business undertaken by them should be disclosed in the 'Notes to Accounts' to their Balance Sheet. A robust internal grievance redressal mechanism is also required to be put in place along with a board-approved customer compensation policy for resolving issues related to services offered. Banks are also to ensure that the insurance companies, whose products are being sold, have robust customer grievance redressal arrangements in place, and at its end, the bank must also facilitate the redressal of grievances of the customer.

The Banking Ombudsman Scheme

The RBI has operationalised a Banking Ombudsman Scheme (BOS) to provide an expeditious and inexpensive forum to bank customers for resolving complaints relating to certain services rendered by banks. The BOS was introduced under Section 35 A of the Banking Regulation Act, 1949 by the RBI with effect from 1995. The Banking Ombudsman (BO) is a senior official appointed by the RBI. He has the responsibility to redress customer complaints against deficiency in certain banking services. All Scheduled Commercial Banks, RRBs and Scheduled Primary (Urban) Co-operative Banks are covered under the scheme.

The BO can receive and consider any complaint relating to a number of deficiencies related to banking operations including Internet banking. The RBI has mentioned a large number of service deficiencies by banks to customers where customers can approach the Ombudsman through a complaint. These include non-payment or inordinate delay in the payment or collection of cheques, drafts, bills, etc.; non-acceptance, without sufficient cause, of small denomination notes tendered for any purpose and for charging of commission in respect thereof; non-acceptance, without sufficient cause, of coins tendered and for charging of commission in respect thereof; non-payment or delay in payment of inward remittances; failure to issue or delay in issue of drafts, pay orders or bankers' cheques; non-adherence to prescribed working hours, etc. A customer can file a complaint before the BO if the bank doesn't give a reply to the customer within a period of one month or the bank rejects the complaint, or if the complainant is not satisfied with the reply given by the bank. Complaints relating to subjects not covered under the scheme can be sent directly to the RBI which processes them departmentally outside the purview of the BO.

The BO has been reaching out to the people in rural areas to spread awareness about the scheme and its usefulness for the customers of banks. In addition to complaints received at the offices of the BO under the BOS, 2006, several complaints relating to customer interfaces with banks not covered under the scheme, as also complaints pertaining to Non-Banking Financial Companies (NBFCs) are received in the RBI, where they get processed in a separate department (The Customer Education and Protection Department) set up for the purpose.

Internal Ombudsmen have also been appointed by commercial banks, following a direction by the RBI. They look into complaints against particular banks. This is expected to result in settlement at the bank level in a majority of complaints and only a few complaints are expected to reach the BO of the RBI.

Other sectoral financial regulators such as IRDA and SEBI have also appointed Ombudsmen to take care of customer grievances relating to their respective sectors. Insurance Ombudsmen are active at the state level and have helped to resolve complaints against insurance companies to a substantial extent.

In fact, as the financial system expands its footprints into the hinterland and includes more and more customers, hitherto excluded for various reasons and as the system tries to promote financial literacy consciously, it is only to be expected that the number of complaints from the users of financial services would increase and that the nature of grievances would also be different.

This is borne by the steady increase in the number of complaints handled by the BO and the increasingly complex cases that the Ombudsmen are required to decide. The volume of complaints received by BO offices increased during 2016-17 by over 27 per cent, from 1,02,000 to 1,30,000[9].

With increasing thrust on digital banking, there is a perceptible shift towards complaints in respect of electronic transactions, whether they are failed transactions at ATMs or fraudulent withdrawals from savings accounts using cloned credit cards. The best thing would be for banks to tone up their operations so that a majority of complaints are addressed at the operating level itself. They would need to sensitise their officials faster and on an ongoing basis so that they are in a position to appreciate the need for true customer service and in the event of something going wrong, they are able to provide some quick solution to the problem. The curriculum in banks' training institutions would require some fine-tuning to include these aspects and the evaluation process of bank officials also would require to take such performances into account.

A strong consumer protection framework in banking and finance not only helps in redressal of consumer grievances as and when they arise but also helps in improving the confidence of people in the system. As regards banking, domestic savers in India still look forward to bank deposits as a safe way of saving one's money. A robust deposit insurance and bank resolution system would certainly strengthen this confidence in the banking system and its regulator and would be useful at a macro-economic level and contribute to financial stability.

Ombudsman for NBFCs

In February 2018, the RBI extended the purview of the Ombudsman Scheme to cover NBFCs and announced that Ombudsmen for NBFCs would be appointed at four metro centres, viz., Chennai,

Kolkata, Mumbai and New Delhi. To begin with, the scheme would cover all deposit-taking NBFCs and based on the experience gained, it would be extended to cover the NBFCs with asset size of Rs 100 crore and above having customer interface.

Ombudsman for the Insurance Sector

In the same manner as customers have complaints against banks, there are many complaints that policy holders have with respect to their insurance policies and most often they don't know where and how to complain. In many cases, people usually let go the claims only because they do not want to get into court cases, which is very expensive and may go on for years. Therefore, to help individuals get their grievances redressed in a quick and cost-effective manner, the Government of India has set up the Insurance Ombudsman Office.

A customer can file complaints with the Ombudsman relating to both life and general insurance policies. Complaints relating to the following can be filed:

a) Any partial or total repudiation of claim by an insurer.
b) Delay in settlement of claims.
c) Non-issuance of policy document after receipt of premium.
d) Any dispute with respect to premium paid or payable in terms of the policy.
e) Any dispute to legal construction of policies insofar as such disputes relate to claims.

Only individuals, not corporates or organisations, can file their complaints in the Ombudsman's office. In case of a complaint, the customer is required to first make a review application with the insurance company's grievance redressal department or the nodal officer appointed for the purpose. Every insurer is mandated to have such a department. If a reply is not received within a period of one month or the reply is not satisfactory, the customer can file a complaint with the Insurance Ombudsman of her jurisdiction. The complaint has to be filed within one year from the final communication from the insurer, after which the complaint would not be entertained. Further, the same complaint should not be pending before any court of law.

After this, a date will be fixed by the Insurance Ombudsman and a personal hearing will be granted to the policy holder. The insurance company is also called in that hearing. An executive from the Ombudsman's office is appointed to represent the policy holder free of charge to help (as the policy holder does not know all the rules of insurance; hence no lawyer is required). The order of the Ombudsman is binding on the insurance company and it cannot challenge the same in a court. However, if the policy holder is not satisfied, she can go ahead and file a case in the court thereafter.

While several steps have been taken by the regulators and the government to address customer grievances in the banking and insurance sectors, the awareness of such measures among rural customers as also the effectiveness of these forums in redressing grievances in the far-flung rural and hilly areas are issues that need to be urgently addressed. The Financial Sector Legislative Reforms Commission (FSLRC), which gave its report to the Government of India in 2013, has, among others, recommended the appointment of financial sector Ombudsmen to take care of customer complaints relating to the financial sector as a whole, and has also recommended that the Ombudsman's office should be set up at the district level so as to provide access to rural customers. Although the recommendation of the Commission has not yet been accepted, there is a strong case for making available a grievance redressal machinery at the district level or at some level which would be closer to rural customers, rather than confining it to the state headquarters.

4

Policy Making – Changing Focus, Adapting to Change

THE rural credit policy in India had at its core the goals of bringing an increasing number of people within the formal financial system and using credit as an instrument of poverty alleviation in conjunction with other measures. The policy orientation was towards increase in supply of credit through expanding outreach of the banking system and adoption of directed credit as a means of financing the hitherto neglected sectors of the economy, called the priority sectors. Much of the financial services provision in rural India, therefore, has been policy-driven, as we have seen in earlier chapters.

The role of banks has been crucial to the processes of giving an impetus to development. The Indian banking system has today an impressive penetrative outreach and there is now a bank branch fulfilling the need of every 8000 people of the population. As a result of these initiatives, there has been a substantial broadening of the infrastructure for credit delivery resulting in increased outreach and reduction in the influence of informal agencies. This is evidenced by the increase in the share of institutional sources in the cash debts of rural households from 7.3 per cent in the early 1950s to 64 per cent in 1991. Although the next survey conducted in 2001 showed that the share of institutional sources had decreased marginally (to 62 per cent)[1]. We have seen in the earlier two chapters how the banking infrastructure in the country has evolved over the years.

Banking is by far the most strictly regulated activity, as banks are the custodians of public money and people need to have faith in the banking system. In India, the twin objectives of bank regulation have been consumer protection and ensuring financial stability. Banking law in the country has laid down the detailed framework and banks must conform to these regulations in order to remain fit and sound and carry on banking activity. However, banks operate in a socio-economic milieu, the stability of which is looked after by the government. Priorities of the government, therefore, have to be kept in view while dealing with banks. Short-term policies are influenced by the government's preferences, while long-term policy measures emanate from the broad policy objectives of the people and the parties in power, subject of course to the systems and procedure followed in a democratic set-up. This approach is applicable to rural finance too. As we have stated earlier, policy making has always been a function of time, place and person. If one of these variables is changed, most likely the policy would be different.

As we have already discussed, commercial banks were literally forced into rural banking in the wake of the first phase of bank nationalisation in the country in 1969. The Branch Licensing Policy adopted by the RBI consciously pushed banks to open branches in rural and semi-urban areas. To be able to open one urban or metropolitan branch, four branches were required to be opened in rural areas. This to a certain extent took care of the supply side and led over time to the establishment of a large network of commercial bank branches in the rural sector.

Over the years, the spread of Automated Teller Machines (ATMs) has also played an important role in enhancing access to banking services. Close to 20 per cent of ATMs, set up by public sector banks, were in rural area as of March 2017, with another 28 per cent being in semi-urban areas[2]. The ATM network, however, generally mirrors the geographical distribution of bank branches and fewer number of ATMs are found in the eastern and north-eastern regions of the country. Wherever they are found, ATMs are generally used for withdrawal of cash from bank accounts. Although they have provision for several other services, these are seldom used. The ATM network actually facilitates more use of cash!

In the context of the financial sector reforms that started in the early 1990s, the approach to rural financial policies has also undergone a gradual shift with more freedom given to banks for selecting borrowers and determining the price of loans and emphasis on the financial health of the institutions purveying credit. The environment in which rural financial institutions operate is changing fast, providing opportunities and throwing up challenges to these institutions to make rural financial intermediation a viable activity. At the time of nationalisation of major commercial banks in 1969 and again in 1980, the policy thrust was undoubtedly in favour of rural and agricultural finance. This had to be provided at any cost, no matter what banks had to do or undergo to ensure this. Subsequently, however, the stand got softened as banks continued to incur losses on unviable operations, predominantly due to overzealous lending in compliance with the norms. The scope of the priority sector was gradually widened to include several emerging areas, ceilings in respect of activities already included under the Priority Sector Lending also were relaxed to include more borrowers. The philosophy now was to see that more money goes into the priority sector, from whom or in what manner became actually immaterial. A mechanism to tap the banks' shortfall in lending to the priority sector or agriculture was put in place. The Rural Infrastructure Development Fund (RIDF) was established with NABARD to assist state governments in completing infrastructure projects, which had been started but were languishing for want of funds. Foreign banks operating in India were asked to park their shortfall in the priority sector lending with SIDBI, the apex financial institution established in 1990 to take care of the MSME (then small scale industries) sector. More freedom was given to banks in deciding on lending rates, as also on the amounts of working capital loans. Internationally accepted prudential norms were implemented in India with the objective of making the banking system stronger and more resilient and more capable of taking on the emerging challenges and risks. The risk management framework was also gradually put in place to equip our banks to more efficiently manage their capital and take informed credit and investment decisions.

The Institutional Design

We have already seen in the previous chapters how a multi-agency system for delivery of rural finance has emerged over a period of time through conscious policy intervention. Starting with the government providing finance to farmers in the form of Taccavi loans, to the establishment of cooperative banks all over the country, roping in commercial banks to facilitate rural finance, nationalisation of major commercial banks, setting up of regional rural banks, creation of NABARD and SIDBI at the apex level for facilitating and monitoring flow of institutional finance to agriculture and the small enterprise sector respectively, experimenting with local area banks, small finance banks and payments banks, we have seen the emergence of various supporting mechanisms leading to the development of a complex eco-system. At the heart of the institutional design has been the pioneering role of the RBI, which is in a unique position among central banks in the world, having an explicit mandate to facilitate flow of rural credit[3]. Since its inception in 1935, the RBI has been playing an active role in the development of an appropriate institutional structure for this purpose. Each stage of institutional development has also been associated with the design of products suitable in the context of a particular institution or of a particular target group.

We have also seen how NABARD upon its creation in 1982, took over a substantial part of the RBI's developmental functions.[3] NABARD's organisational character and its functions have undergone changes over time. Its financial and developmental roles have been under focus and expectations of the Government and the public from NABARD are on the rise.

Priority Sector Lending

A policy of directed lending in the form of Priority Sector Lending (PSL) was put in place in the aftermath of bank nationalisation, with the priority sector defined to include those hitherto neglected sectors of the economy, where bank finance was necessary, but not forthcoming. The description of the priority sector for bank finance was formalised in 1972 and guidelines were issued on the scope of the priority sector on the basis of the report submitted by an Informal Study Group on Statistics relating to the priority sectors constituted by the RBI. In November 1974, banks were advised to raise the share of the priority sectors in their aggregate advances to 33.3 per cent by March 1979. The target was raised to 40 per cent in March 1980, to be achieved by banks by March 1985. The present framework of the PSL is based on the report of the working group on the PSL and the 20-Point Economic Programme (Chairman: Dr K. S. Krishnaswamy). Since then there have been several changes in the scope of the priority sector as also in the targeting system for banks but the directed credit mechanism continues to function[4].

According to the present PSL norms, scheduled commercial banks have to provide 40 per cent of their loans (measured in terms of Adjusted Net Bank Credit or ANBC) to the identified priority sectors in accordance with the RBI regulations, with sub-targets made applicable for lending to agriculture and weaker sections. The PSL, which could perhaps have continued to be a simple proportion of total bank credit extended to various sectors, has over the years become too complicated, with the denominator of the ratio (ANBC or Credit Equivalent of Off-Balance Sheet Exposure, whichever is higher) undergoing several changes and itself becoming a difficult concept for a layman to understand.

Although the PSL concept has continued over the years, both the composition of the priority sector and the targeting system have undergone several changes. The latest comprehensive revision in the PSL norms was announced based on the recommendations of the RBI Internal Working Group on PSL, which gave its report in March 2015[5]. Changes in classification of the priority sectors and targets were also made as per the new norms. Following are the main categories of the priority sector along with the target and sub-targets (credit percentages are expressed in terms of ANBC or Credit Equivalent Amount of Off-Balance Sheet Exposure, whichever is higher):

Overall priority sector: 40 per cent

Agriculture: 18 per cent; within the 18 per cent target for agriculture, a target of 8 per cent of ANBC is prescribed for lending to small and marginal farmers.

Micro Enterprises: 7.5 per cent (There is no target for lending to the MSME sector as a whole.)

Export: Incremental export credit up to 2 per cent for domestic banks and foreign banks with 20 branches and above.

Education: Loans to individuals for educational purposes including vocational courses up to Rs 10 lakh.

Housing: Loans to individuals up to Rs 28 lakh in metropolitan centres (with population of 10 lakh and above) and loans up to Rs 20 lakh in other centres for purchase/construction of a dwelling unit per family.

Social Infrastructure: Bank loans up to a limit of Rs 5 crore per borrower for building social infrastructure for activities, namely schools, healthcare facilities, drinking water facilities and sanitation facilities in Tier II to Tier VI centres (centres having population less than 1 lakh).

Renewable Energy: Bank loans up to a limit of Rs 15 crore to borrowers (individual households – Rs 10 lakh) including for public utilities, viz., street lighting systems and remote village electrification.

Others: Self Help Groups (SHGs), Joint Liability Groups (JLGs) etc.

From the above categories, a sub-category of 'weaker sections' has also been identified so that they can get special preference under the PSL. Weaker sections comprise the wheel within the wheel as it were and form the core of the priority sector, which actually needs priority tag for bank finance. The regulations stipulate that banks should give 10 per cent of their ANBC to weaker sections, which include small and marginal farmers, artisans, village and cottage industries with a credit limit up to Rs 1 lakh, beneficiaries of certain government-sponsored schemes, SC/STs, SHGs, persons with disabilities, overdrafts up to Rs 5,000 in the PMJDY accounts, distressed persons, individual women beneficiaries up to Rs 1 lakh and beneficiaries of differential rate of interest scheme.

Several important changes were made in the revised PSL norms in the light of the Internal Working Group (IWG) recommendations.[5] New categories, viz., medium enterprises, social infrastructure and renewable energy were included as part of the redefined priority sector. A separate target for small and marginal farmers (8 per cent) and micro enterprises (7.5 per cent) and inclusion of food and agro-processing units under agriculture were the other major changes. From 2016-17 onwards, the priority sector achievement of banks is assessed on the quarterly average basis instead of the annual basis as earlier.

In the wake of the securities scam of 1991-92, the RBI introduced a scheme of penalty for foreign banks, which did not meet the then PSL target of 32 per cent or the sub-targets in respect of small-scale industries and exports, as applicable at that time. Foreign banks were asked to deposit the shortfall in lending to the priority sector with the Small Industries Development Bank of India (SIDBI). Subsequently, the system of asking banks to deposit the shortfall or a part thereof was made applicable to domestic banks too and in 2004-05, domestic scheduled commercial banks having shortfall in lending to the priority sector/sub-sectors vis-a-vis the stipulated targets, were asked to deposit amounts proportional to the shortfall with NABARD, in the Rural Infrastructure Development Fund (RIDF). The policy has continued year after year and the domestic scheduled commercial banks are now required to contribute to the RIDF and similar funds set up with NABARD, SIDBI and National Housing Bank (NHB), as announced by the Government of India in the Finance Minister's Budget speech.

Another important modification in the PSL, made by the RBI after the recommendations of the IWG-relates to foreign banks. Foreign banks with 20 branches and above already have PSL targets of 40 per cent and sub-targets for agriculture and weaker sections. These targets were required to be achieved by 31 March, 2018 as per the action plans approved by the RBI. Foreign banks with less than 20 branches would also now move to the total priority sector target of 40 per cent by 2019-20. The sub-target for the MSME sector would be included for them in 2018.

A far-reaching modification to the PSL framework for banks is the introduction of the Priority Sector Lending Certificates (PSLC). PSLCs were conceived as a mechanism to facilitate the flow of credit to the identified priority sectors by rewarding banks, which overshot the achievement of the targets, at the same time giving an option to banks, which fell short of the targets. Banks lending more than the stipulated minimum target (overall priority sector, agriculture, weaker sections, small and marginal farmers, micro-enterprises) were allowed to issue PSLCs which could be purchased by banks having shortfall at market determined rates. The idea of PSLC was originally mooted in the report of the Committee on Financial Sector Reforms, headed by Dr Raghuram Rajan (2008), but was not initially found implementable. The scheme that was put in place in April 2016 used the core banking network of the RBI (named as E-Kuber) and provided a platform for selling and buying PSLCs. As stated in an RBI Annual Report, this allowed the market mechanism to drive the PSL by leveraging on the comparative strength of banks in lending to various segments included in the priority sector. As per the RBI, the total trade value of PSLCs was Rs 498 billion during 2016-17.

There has been criticism that PSLCs encourage sort of 'lazy banking', as banks, which are not able to achieve their targets, can always invest in PSLCs and get away with it. But in this criticism, one fact often ignored is that the system is confined to banks only. PSLCs are issued by banks, which have lent more than the targeted amount to agriculture and other sectors. These banks have been incentivised to lend more to these sectors by the PSLC mechanism, in the absence of which there would be no incentive for them to lend more and simple achievement of the specified target would be enough. Although the regulation is the same for all banks in the system, it is well known that all banks do not have the same level of potential or capability to handle a given sector. Some banks have the capacity to lend more to, say, agriculture, as compared to other banks and the PSLC provides them the mechanism, which supports this type of 'lending beyond the targets'. The price of PSLC is market determined. If another bank sees it worthwhile to invest in PSLC and achieve the target, so be it. It, therefore, makes more sense to have such a system, which incentivises lending and quickly results in flow of more credit to the sector, rather than having a system of penalty such as deposits under the RIDF, where the results would show after considerable time and there is no guarantee that more credit would flow to the sector as a result of this provision.

An issue, which is often raised in the context of the PSL and lending under various schemes of the Government, relates to Non-Performing Assets (NPAs) in the priority sector loans. The gross

NPAs of the banking system in India, which were 2.3 per cent of the total loans in March 2008, increased to 9.6 per cent of the total loans in March 2017[6]. If we add to it the loans restructured by banks, the stressed assets of the banking system would be much higher. This has led to lending paralysis, a condition in which bankers shy away from taking decisions on lending for fear of accumulating more bad loans. It is true that NPAs are not peculiar to the priority sector and that credit risk crystallising in the form of NPAs exists in all segments to varying degrees. In fact, as per the RBI report on Trend and Progress of Banking in India, more than three-fourths of the delinquent loans were concentrated in the non-priority sector, with industries recording the highest level of NPAs, followed by the infrastructure sector. However, given the fact that this lending activity is mainly policy-driven and not exactly as per the own commercial judgement of banks and that the segments usually call for some soft handling because of their sensitive nature, NPAs in these segments assume a different colour. Banks being commercial entities will lend anyway; but when forced to lend to some sectors or some type of borrowers and when they are pulled up for not lending and penalised, in tangible or non-tangible terms, the lending process may get vitiated and as a result, repayment of loans gets affected. The level of NPAs in the agriculture sector is about 5 per cent of the loan outstanding, while in the MSME sector, it is around 8 per cent. In the case of agriculture, a case has been made in some states for banks and government agencies to jointly monitor utilisation and repayment of loans. Joint recovery groups with bankers and local government officials have also been set up in several states and districts but the effectiveness of these approaches has been limited. Like many other initiatives, this is also more dependent on the people involved than the system. Similar is the case with small industrial units, although here bankers have a recourse to the SARFAESI Act as well as other soft and hard recovery measures. The result is more often than not unsatisfactory.

Some banks have been resorting to securitisation of assets under priority sector loans, and also if the loans turn non-performing, to sale of loans to Asset Reconstruction Companies (ARCs), who ultimately take the responsibility to follow up and recover the dues from the borrowers. The argument for the latter is that as the system grows, specialised institutions or agencies who can manage certain functions better than others, specialising in certain activities, come in. Seen in this context, ARCs are an extended arm of the banking system. But the problem is, when someone believes his job is to lend and then either sell off by way of securitisation or ultimately hive off the portfolio for sale to ARCs, the issue of moral hazard comes into play. The traditional view of a bank that works for giving a loan and also for recovering it from the borrower, seems to have a lot of merit. In the anxiety for achieving specialisation, we have forgotten the basics that drive the business of banking. This seems to be the problem that led to the global financial crisis of the last decade. If another institution like ARC can do it, why not the bank itself? Why can't the bank develop the required expertise and employ the right kind of people who would specialise in loan recovery? Surely, development of in-house expertise in loan recovery would address the moral hazard issue involved, when a bank only originates the loan and at a later date when it becomes NPA, transfers it to another company.

Another similar problematic area is that of education loans, a thrust area for the government, given its desire to ensure that as many Indians get educated as possible and be a part of the PSL. According to the Indian Banks Association[7], NPAs in education loans rose to 7.7 per cent in the financial year 2016-17 from 5.7 per cent two years ago. In view of this, the government needs to think as to what extent it should be pressurising banks to give such loans, As per the guidelines, loans up to Rs 4 lakh are given without collateral securities. Even for ensuring that no poor student gets left behind due to the lack of funds, the government could try to come up with some innovative solutions. There is a credit guarantee scheme operating now through the National Credit Guarantee Trustee

Company (NCGTC), a private limited company set up by the Department of Financial Services to take care of credit guarantee funds for various purposes, as per the policies of the government. However, it is too early to see the results.

Coming to the affordable housing scheme of the Government of India, which is also under the priority sector, given the employment benefits from housing construction, apart from the fact that several million houses will get constructed, the scheme is a welcome one. NPAs in the overall housing loan sector were around 1.1 per cent in 2016-17. But for loans less than Rs 2 lakh, the NPA levels are a whopping 10.4 per cent, making it clear that this group of home-owners lack the wherewithal to fund their loans despite the loan being subsidised[8]. While the government needs to decide on whether such loans are viable, if it does decide to continue, it is only fair that it compensates banks for NPAs in some way.

Sometimes, one is tempted to ask, what would happen if the PSL targets are withdrawn? The simple answer is, we do not know. There is a view that but for the strict guidelines and vigilant enforcement, rural banking would perhaps have remained mere tokenism. It has been an assumption, which is of course based on our observations in the past, that given a choice, banks, which are commercial organisations, would not lend to these areas, which today constitute the priority sector, to the desired extent. We do not know whether banks, which have opened a vast network of branches in rural and semi-urban areas, would reduce lending to agriculture, if tomorrow the 18 per cent target is withdrawn, or reduced. It is the fear that banks may not lend as much to these sectors in the absence of specific targets that has made these targets 'holy cows', which cannot even be debated about in public, forget reduction or elimination. In fact, the Committee on the Financial System (Narasimham Committee I) had recommended that the priority sector be redefined and focused only on the core area, which constitutes weaker sections, and a revised target of 10 per cent of net bank credit be fixed for the redefined priority sector. But then this was a major recommendation of the Committee which was not accepted by the government.

Financing Agriculture

The rural economy in India has been traditionally equated with agriculture. It has been the most important economic activity in our country and even today, it contributes around 14 per cent of the Gross Domestic Product (GDP) and directly or indirectly provides employment to half of the country's population. The word 'agriculture' actually connotes a spectrum, on the one end of which lies subsistence agriculture, cultivation by farm labourers, landless tenant farmers, marginal farmers and small farmers. On the other end of the spectrum lies commercial farming engaged by large farmers and corporate farmers. No wonder, agricultural development with its various linkages, backward and forward, has been a highly complex issue. Each part of the spectrum requires a different strategy and a different approach for development. Similarly, financing agriculture would also necessitate different strategies and approaches for different parts of the spectrum. The strategy for financing of medium and large farmers would not work when it comes to financing of small and marginal farmers. It is generally true that the most financially excluded are those lying at the lower end of the spectrum – the people of small means and those having very low level of asset holding.

The National Agriculture Policy (NAP), 2002 envisages a growth rate of over 4 per cent per annum. While the ground level credit flow to agriculture has been steadily growing over the years and has reached a level of over Rs 9,50,000 crore during the year 2016-17, a large increase in credit, particularly investment credit, would be required to improve capital formation in agriculture and help achieve the growth rate envisaged in the NAP on a continuous basis. The roots of rural and agricultural crisis lie in structural problems –

fragmentation of land holdings, lack of land-leasing laws, market imperfections, lack of access to markets and lack of adequate risk mitigation mechanisms in farming. Other major challenges that need to be addressed in this regard would include improving lending to small and marginal farmers with scattered land holdings, developing suitable risk mitigation mechanism and diversification of agriculture away from a predominantly cereal-based cultivation to value-added, commercial agriculture, at the same time taking care of marginal sections such as landless labourers and tenant farmers. The whole agricultural value chain has to be strengthened – starting from provision of inputs to actual production of crops, harvesting and post-harvest operations, every part needs to be focused to ensure sustainable operations and to see that the farmers' income keeps pace with the changing times.

Banks in India have been providing financial assistance to agriculture in a conducive policy environment, as we have seen in the earlier chapters. The necessary systems and processes have been put in place over a period of time. In fact, finance is the life blood of agricultural operations and the farmer, being the entrepreneur who faces all the risks in the occupation, needs regular and assured doses of credit to keep the operations going. Unfortunately, even after decades of planning and policy focus, a sizeable number of farmers are still outside the purview of institutional finance and this is exacerbated by the distress that a section of farmers faces, which in some cases leads to farmers committing suicide. As per the National Sample Survey Office (NSSO) Situational Assessment of Farmers, 2013, the proportion of farmers who did not benefit by the formal financial institutions was as high as 51 per cent.

Herein lies one of the biggest challenges of financial inclusion in our country. While more and more people have been covered under bank finance for agriculture, the number of people who stand excluded is so large that a fundamental shift in perception and practice is required to bridge the gap. Financial institutions in the country seem to be following what a writer calls the cafeteria approach, viz., provide services that are available on the menu. There is hardly any customisation to suit the needs of the target groups. This exclusive supply side focus has made agricultural credit unresponsive to actual production, productivity or income of farmers. Cooperative banks and societies, which were once seen to be farmer-friendly and which accounted for a large proportion of institutional finance, have lost out as their health has been deteriorating and putting them back on the rails seems to be an uphill task. As commercial banks rapidly take their place and continue to extend substantial amounts of finance for agricultural operations, their approaches are expected to change to align with farmers' needs and the contours of the ever-increasing complexities of agriculture. Even today, when the farmer stands at the centre of policy support to agriculture, anecdotal evidence shows that he is not dealt with properly by the mainstream banking system, which leads to a lot of heart-burn and forces the farmer to tap the so called non-institutional sources, friends, relatives, moneylenders, etc., often with disastrous consequences for himself and for agriculture as a whole.

Farmers' suicide is a highly complex socio-economic issue that has engaged the attention of the country for several years now. While the governments, both at the Centre as well as the states concerned, have generally been taking a stand that steps are being taken to address the issues and that whatever needs to be done is being done, there is an undercurrent of public feeling that the core issues are not being tackled properly. Policy patchwork to manage the aftermath of unpleasant happenings is seldom an alternative to a well thought out inclusive growth strategy to improve the lives of farmers across the spectrum. For decades, the country has been witnessing debates and discussions on how to improve the agricultural ecosystem and to help farmers in times of need or of adverse climate or market impact. Governments cutting across political parties have held out promises to prioritise the farmers' development but the result is that we keep discussing the same issues and problems again and again, keep moving in circles, as the condition of farmers in several parts of the country deteriorates and they are forced to take the extreme step.

The distortion of the rural credit system is one of the problems that has roots at the policy making level and its impact is felt all over. The targeting approach for banks in financing the priority sector including agriculture has perhaps been an easy way to force money into the system and has seldom encouraged banks to study the needs of the system properly. In our concern for the 'letters' of the rules governing the PSL, we have forgotten the 'spirit' behind the rules and mere achievement of targets is celebrated, without analysing the manner in which targets are achieved and studying the benefits accruing to the system as a result of the increase of financial assistance. We are bent upon influencing the interest rates charged by banks while extending loans and we feel that loans to farmers have to be cheap, like several other inputs, which are subsidised but we fail to appreciate that the availability of adequate credit is of prime importance and the local moneylender is an important link in this process. A few percentage points variation in interest rates actually does not matter much unless interest rates are usurious. We force banks to lend at relatively low rates, force them to achieve the targets set by us and expect them to be exemplary bankers, providing timely and adequate credit to agriculture, monitor the end use of credit and ensure recovery in a climate vitiated by frequent promises of loan waivers. Not surprisingly, bank credit has grown manifold, while production has improved slowly and productivity has remained almost constant. The real income of farmers has not kept pace with the increase in costs and inflation and has led the government to prioritise doubling of farmers' income in about seven years. The terms of trade have generally been unfavourable for agriculture and if we compare agriculture as an occupation with other occupations, their risk-return profile and income generating capacity, it won't be difficult to understand why around 40 per cent of farmers would, given a choice, leave agriculture[9], or why the farmer's son is no more interested in continuing in agriculture. Mere romanticising of agriculture is not enough; practical issues crave urgent attention.

The Kisan Credit Card (KCC) scheme has been a significant innovation in the dispensation of agricultural credit and has provided the much-needed flexibility to farmers in drawing credit and making repayments depending on their cash flows. The scheme, which was first implemented through guidelines issued by NABARD and the RBI in the year 1998, has undergone several changes from time to time in response to perceived needs as also recommendations of various study reports and committee reports. The latest comprehensive revision was made in 2012, which allowed banks to issue KCCs for five years, include part of investment credit as also consumption credit in the overall limit sanctioned and to allow increase in the limit every year by 10 per cent to take care of the increasing cost of farming. Keeping in view the progress of digital technology, it had also become necessary to issue KCCs in the form of 'RuPay smart cards', which the farmers could use to withdraw money at ATMs. The KCC scheme has been the subject of several research and study proposals and the general impression is that the scheme has served its purpose well but improvements are necessary both in the delivery of credit through this mechanism as well as in improving financial literacy of farmers, who being smart-KCC holders also need to be well aware of its methods of operation. The scheme must be seen and utilised as a cash credit system, farmers drawing cash whenever required and depositing any surplus they may have, rather than withdrawing the entire sanctioned amount at a time, which also helps to some extent in the diversion of funds for other purposes, money being fungible. Educating farmers on how to use KCCs properly should have been among the first priorities of the banking system, as also of the government but even after close to two decades of operation, a significant percentage of farmers withdraw the entire year's requirement in one or two installments[10], showing that they do not understand the basics of a KCC. This perhaps speaks volumes of the supply side weaknesses. Implementation-level issues are not taken care of while designing a scheme. Maybe policy makers take a view that once the scheme is in operation, things would take care of themselves and start showing results. In reality, this does not happen.

Although commercial banks' lending to agriculture has substantially increased over time and a large network of branches is engaged in delivery of agricultural credit, the issue of bank officials not having the right 'attitude' towards farmers is often highlighted, so much so that even banks themselves believe in this. Banks have tried all sorts of experiments, including recruiting of agriculture specialists, setting up of dedicated training institutions to impart periodical trainings to staff, partnering with specialised external institutions and adopting a focus on agriculture and rural finance at the top-level discussions. In spite of all this, the complaint persists. The press also gives its views on this while analysing cases of farmers' suicides or other forms of agrarian distress. Although farmers' suicides is a complex phenomenon and needs proper understanding of the socio-economic backdrop and also personal problems of the person concerned, generally it is understood that indebtedness and pressure from lenders contributes to this unfortunate outcome. Even when indebtedness is to moneylenders or other non-institutional sources, the issue often flagged is non-availability of financial assistance from banks, which led to the farmer approaching a moneylender in the first place. As we have repeatedly seen earlier in this book, expectations from the banking sector are on the rise and whenever there is a gap in delivery or in meeting these expectations, banks come for very harsh treatment.

The Government of India has been fixing targets for lending by banks to agriculture during a financial year and announcing in the

Budget speech of the Finance Minister. This is in addition to the PSL target. However, while the priority sector targets are specified as percentages to outstanding loans, the annual target set by the government is a target for disbursement during the year. Like many other targets set by the government, our banking system has been achieving these annual targets without fail, a situation which has been prompting the government to increase the target in quantitative terms every year, by adding an arbitrary amount. For 2018-19, the target has been set at Rs 11 lakh crore, a 10 per cent increase from Rs 10 lakh crore set during the previous year. The Government's intentions are very clear and the objective is to give a boost to agricultural finance. In the anxiety for achieving multiple targets, banks seldom think beyond the distribution of this huge credit flow across segments in the agricultural sector and the outcome of such massive lending – its translation into some tangible increase in production or productivity or in farmers' income has not been monitored with the same enthusiasm.

Another area where the Government has been taking active interest is in the interest rates charged by banks on agricultural loans. With deregulation of the financial sector in the early 1990s, slowly the policy of dictating interest rates to be charged by banks was given a go by and banks were allowed to stipulate their interest rates to all sectors, including agriculture. This was, of course, subject to broad policy guidelines set by the RBI. There is, however, a strong feeling among many people, particularly those in the government that credit has to be given at low rates to farmers. In a deregulated scenario, this translated into the funding of interest charged by banks to farmers by the government. The Interest Subvention Scheme (ISS) was implemented by the government in 2006, under which banks were required to give crop loans to farmers up to Rs 3 lakh at only 7 per cent per annum and the government undertook to reimburse banks 2 per cent, so that such loans would actually fetch 9 per cent to financing banks. This was a blanket decision and did not in any manner factor in banks' cost of funds or any other costs that normally determine interest rates on loans given by banks. Since the government was playing its ownership card in bringing in such a regulation, the scheme was made applicable to public sector banks only. Although private sector banks were subject to the same agricultural lending target and had to compete with public sector banks even in the rural and agricultural sector, the subvention scheme was not extended to them, until much later in 2012, when a decision was taken by the government to include agricultural loans issued by private sector banks in their rural and semi-urban branches for providing interest subvention. As things stand now, the Government of India is providing 2 per cent subvention to banks for crop loans on the condition that banks would lend at 7 per cent. A further subvention of 3 per cent is given to farmers who repay their loans in time, thus bringing down the interest cost for them to only 4 per cent. Some state governments have gone ahead and provided additional subventions in respect of agricultural loans, over and above the Central Government stipulations. In Andhra Pradesh and Telangana, farmers get crop loans up to Rs 1 lakh interest-free (*vaddi leni runalu*) and for loans up to Rs 3 lakh, there is a system of *pavla vaddi,* under which farmers pay only 3 per cent interest per annum.

Apart from putting pressure on banks' financials, limiting subvention only to crop loans serves as a perverse incentive for farmers to go only for crop loans from banks, as in the absence of any such facility in the case of term loans or investment loans, the farmer is not interested in taking those loans. In a situation when there is an emergent need to improve investment credit in agriculture, which would lead to more asset creation, anecdotal evidence also shows that crop loans have been diverted for procuring assets, for which normally a term loan should have been taken. It seems peculiar that when the entire system talks of enhancing investment credit in agriculture, the government thinks it appropriate to continue with interest subvention only in respect of crop loans.

While institutional credit to the agriculture sector has steadily improved, credit flow to small and marginal farmers has been a matter of particular concern. Small and marginal farmers who comprise around 85 per cent of all land holdings in the country, with significant local variations among states and regions, have been traditionally treated as part of weaker sections under the priority sector for bank lending. They need substantial credit support for land development, intensive cultivation, introduction of high-value crops, water management and allied activities. But it is this group of farmers that has lost out on farm sector policies in the past, whether it is for cultivation or extension services or crop insurance. Studies have shown that small and marginal farmers depend more on wage income than income from cultivation. In the revised PSL guidelines issued by the RBI in 2015, a sub-target of 7.5 per cent of net bank credit has been stipulated for commercial banks and regional rural banks for extending credit to small and marginal farmers. But as we have seen above, it is not target achievement through more credit alone which will improve the lot of these people, but simultaneous efforts must be made by all stakeholders, primarily the government, to facilitate necessary linkages and provide adequate insurance. Being small players, these are a highly vulnerable group in agriculture.

Another group of farmers, who are perhaps the most vulnerable in agriculture, are tenant farmers, who do not have land of their own, and who cultivate on the lands of others, mostly leased out to them orally. Access to finance for farming purposes has been a nightmare for them, not only because they have no record of cultivating land but also because of the fact that many of the landowners actually avail farm loans on the basis of land records. Admittedly, this is a complex socio-economic issue which needs to be tackled at various levels. Banks have found out a way to lend to them, mostly through Joint Liability Groups (JLGs). The RBI and the Government of India have also been advocating this mode of credit delivery to landless tenant farmers. One particular innovation, made in Andhra Pradesh in 2011, however, needs special mention. The state government enacted the Andhra Pradesh Land Licensed Cultivators Act, 2011 and started issuing Loan Eligibility Cards (LECs) to tenant farmers in 2012. The cards were valid for a period of one year and could be renewed thereafter. Banks were required to provide loans to tenant farmers on the basis of these LEC cards. Loans up to Rs 50,000 were to be given without any collateral. Although this was a novel idea, and the state government's intervention had the potential to ensure credit flow to tenant farmers without any difficulty, implementation issues soon emerged. Banks found it difficult to lend to tenant farmers in cases where landowners had already availed of finance and in cases where loans were extended by banks on the strength of LECs, the overdue and NPA became high. Further, from the government's side, the cards were valid for only one year and renewal could not be ensured before the crop season, making it difficult for banks to lend. After some initial success, that too in some districts, the LEC Scheme did not really take off.

Agriculture, in its broad definition, includes horticulture, animal husbandry, forestry, dairy and poultry farming, pisciculture and other allied activities[11]. In addition to cultivation of crops, activities allied to agriculture also play an important role in the rural economy. Bank finance for these activities is generally not a problem, though in several cases, selection of a borrower in a village with the right inclination and experience to carry out a certain activity can be tricky. There are quite a few schemes implemented by the Government of India and state governments as well as by NABARD. Banks themselves also have schemes for lending to the allied sectors. These activities not only supplement farmers' income but also provide a much needed cushion to farmers in agriculturally lean years, and also in the event of crops getting damaged due to natural calamities or local disturbances and help farmers overcome agrarian distress to some extent. Loans to these allied sectors are generally term loans and are of higher amounts. As such, these loans need to be appraised properly as per banks' established systems. In these cases, as we have seen, there is no concession available to borrowers in matters of interest rates, but capital subsidy is sometimes available under schemes which are implemented by the government.

Crop Insurance – Managing Production Risk in Agriculture

Agriculture is admittedly one of the riskiest enterprises in the country, as several factors, which decide the crop output or price, are beyond the control of small entrepreneurs, that is, farmers. The farmer has learnt to manage some of the lesser risks, those associated with himself or his family, but for managing bigger risks such as natural calamities, pest attack, market fluctuations, etc., he needs support from the state. India has been experimenting with crop insurance since the early 1970s and every three to four years, an updated version of the scheme emerges. Nevertheless, it is common understanding that we have not been able to address production risk in agriculture in a comprehensive manner.

The Pradhan Mantri Fasal Bima Yojana (the Prime Minister's Crop Insurance Scheme), which is in existence now, aims to provide insurance coverage and financial support to farmers in the event of failure of any of the notified crops as a result of natural calamities, pests and diseases, stabilise the income of farmers to ensure their continuance in farming, encourage farmers to adopt innovative and modern agricultural practices and in the process, to help ensure flow of credit to the agriculture sector. This scheme, an improvement over the earlier scheme, National Agricultural Insurance Scheme or Rashtriya Krishi Bima Yojana, is designed to help in decreasing the burden of premiums on farmers who take loans for their cultivation and to safeguard them against inclement weather. The claim settlement process has also been made simpler and faster in the new scheme.

All farmers including sharecroppers and tenant farmers growing the notified crops in the notified areas are eligible for coverage under the PMFBY. Non-loanee farmers are required to submit necessary documentary evidence of land records prevailing in the State Records of Right (RoR), Land Possession Certificate (LPC), etc. All farmers availing Seasonal Agricultural Operations (SAO) loans from financial institutions (i.e. loanee farmers) for the notified crops are covered compulsorily. While the scheme is optional for non-loanee farmers, special efforts are required to be made to ensure maximum coverage of SC, ST and women farmers under the scheme, and Panchayati Raj Institutions (PRIs) may be involved for the implementation and also for obtaining farmers' feedback[12].

The scheme is implemented on an 'area approach' basis, for each notified crop, for widespread calamities. The assumption that all the insured farmers, in a unit of insurance, defined as 'Notified Area' for a crop, face similar risk exposures, incur to a large extent identical cost of production per hectare, earn comparable farm income per hectare, and experience similar extent of crop loss due to the operation of an insured peril in the notified area. The unit of insurance can be demographically mapped with a region having homogeneous risk profile for the notified crop.

While the overall control on the implementation of the scheme by insurance companies lies with the Ministry of Agriculture, the Ministry has designated the Agriculture Insurance Company (AIC) and some private sector insurance companies to participate in operationalisation of the crop insurance scheme. The choice of the private company is, however, left to the states, with the condition that there would be one insurance company for the whole state.

With the implementation of the PMFBY, some irritants existing in earlier schemes have been removed. However, it is to be seen to what extent it addresses the issue of agrarian distress and helps in de-risking agriculture appropriately. Its effectiveness can be judged only after one observes its operations over a few crop cycles. In the earlier crop insurance scheme, small and marginal farmers seem to have been largely left out, as pointed out in a report from the Comptroller and Auditor General of India (CAG) in 2017[13].

In an assessment of the PMFBY, renowned agricultural scientists Dr Ashok Gulati and Dr Siraj Hussain point to several administrative glitches and the typical red tape that "does not inspire confidence with farmers as they have to wait for months, and even years, to be compensated for their losses." Further, performance under the scheme has not been uniform across states. In some states, significant delays have been observed even in the selection of the insurance company[14].

Another study conducted in Telangana observes that "unless the whole scheme of insurance is recorded to suit the specific requirements of the state, this would not be beneficial. The scheme could benefit irrigated tracts and not drought-affected farmers. Farmers also desired that claims should be assessed individual farmer-wise and not village-wise"[15].

The above analysis shows that lack of coherent and consistent policies and sub-optimal implementation of policies has to a great extent affected agriculture development in the country. There is no dearth of policy or of programmes but the agriculture sector has suffered from ad-hocism and myopic decision making, often tagging the sector to political vicissitudes. As a result, risk in the sector has amplified and the situation has come to such a pass that many farmers, given a chance, would like to leave agriculture. Agrarian distress in the country is often over-simplified by some as something related to non-availability of institutional credit. More than credit, it needs action on other fronts in the agricultural value chain, such as proper inputs like seeds, fertiliser and water, extension technology, post-harvest operations including storage, transport and processing, wherever required, as also marketing of the produce. Several forces that influence the viability of agriculture as an economic activity are at play. Most of these actions are beyond the scope of financial institutions and lie in the domain of government action.

Agriculture in our country has always suffered because of natural calamities, such as heavy rains and floods, cyclones, tsunamis and droughts. Farmers have been subjected to severe strain and have lost their assets, including standing crops, sometimes repeatedly over several consecutive years. Their capacity to pay back bank loans has been severely eroded. Banks are under obligation to provide some relief measures in the case of natural calamities, which include restructuring or rescheduling of loans, granting fresh crop loans and additional loans for consumption purposes. This is an automatic process, as per standing guidelines issued by the RBI to banks in this regard, and the forums under the Lead Bank Scheme – the DCC and the SLBC – are activated immediately in case of occurrence of calamities to decide on the action to be followed. The role of the state government is critical in such situations, as it has to declare the place as calamity affected after it has assessed the damage caused by the calamity and banks are required to act in close coordination with the government machinery. Sometimes, when the calamity is prolonged or occurs over two or more years in quick succession, the impact on the farmer is severe. The rescheduled loans and fresh loans build up substantially to multiply his indebtedness, which will often be impossible to meet out of a subsequent year's income. The insurance system is anything but robust. In such cases, there is no recourse for the affected farmer, except perhaps in the form of loan waivers that keep getting announced from time to time in various states and also in the country as a whole. There have been recommendations in some reports[16] about setting up a fund to make payments to banks in such cases. The fund could be set up by the Central Government if necessary with support from state governments and banks and financial institutions, who have a major stake in this process. But for some reason, the recommendation has not been accepted and the situation remains where it was a decade earlier.

Finance for Rural Infrastructure

Infrastructure development is the sine qua non of any sustained development agenda. Apart from large infrastructure projects relating to irrigation, power generation and supply, roads and highways, railways and airports, etc., small infrastructural gaps also adversely affect development. Rural development has suffered in the past and continues to suffer at present primarily due to such infrastructure gaps in rural areas, which has also adversely impacted credit absorption capacity and resulted in low growth. Improvement in rural infrastructure, such as roads and bridges, scientific water management, warehousing, cold storages, provision of marketing facilities including establishment of market-yards, etc. will go a long way in improving farming in the areas concerned, improving credit utilisation and the repaying capacity of borrowers, thus making rural credit a viable and bankable economic proposition. The absence of a patch of an all-weather road or a bridge connecting villages on the two sides of a river, are infrastructural gaps which must be urgently addressed. Their impact on rural development can be immense.

A step has been taken in this direction by setting up the Rural Infrastructure Development Fund (RIDF) with NABARD in 1994-95. Starting with a corpus fund of Rs 2000 crore, to help state governments in the completion of ongoing projects relating to rural infrastructure and funded by banks having shortfall in lending to the priority sector or agriculture, the RIDF has continued to be operational for 23 years. Over the years, its scope has been widened to include financing of social infrastructure projects as well, such as construction of primary school buildings. The Fund has served the twin objectives of helping rural infrastructure and also acting as a punitive measure for banks which failed to achieve the target for the PSL and the sub-target for lending to agriculture. The punitive element lay in the very low interest rates paid to banks by NABARD on the deposits made in the Fund, which are typically for around seven years. Interest rates on the deposits made by banks are inversely related to the shortfall in achieving the agricultural lending target of 18 per cent of adjusted net bank credit, as per the priority sector finance norms.

State governments or state-sponsored organisations formulate proposals and forward them to NABARD for approval, which makes a thorough appraisal and sanctions projects for assistance under the RIDF. Implementation of projects is also monitored by NABARD jointly with the state government. A large number of small-size projects have been assisted under the Fund during the last 23 years. Non-achievement of targets has been the source of RIDF funding and with some banks not being able to achieve targets, the government continues to make announcements about new tranches every year. Utilisation of the Fund, however, needs to be substantially stepped up. As against the aggregate corpus of Rs 2,92,500 crore under various tranches of the RIDF, the cumulative amount disbursed under all the tranches was of the order of Rs. 2,15,605 crore at the end of March 2017[17]. Utilisation is not uniform across states. It has been poor in states where infrastructure development has been traditionally at a low level. However, it is not clear as to whether the banking system has been able to take advantage of the development of rural infrastructure supported by the RIDF in their areas of operation. Project implementation under the RIDF needs to be dovetailed with development plans as well as credit plans of each district to take advantage of the assets created. Various monitoring forums under the LBS must focus on the infrastructure created with the RIDF assistance. The impact studies commissioned by NABARD have validated the positive impact on rural income levels, diversified livelihood activities, improved quality of life, as also positive effect on rural banking.

Financing of Micro, Small and Medium Enterprises

After agriculture, which supports the largest workforce in the country, comes the Micro, Small and Medium Enterprises (MSME) sector, which has in 2016 contributed around 8 per cent of GDP, 45 per cent of exports and employed around 117 million people. A predominantly large percentage of the MSME sector, 94 per cent, comprises micro enterprises, those with original investment in plant and machinery up to Rs 2.5 million, if it is a manufacturing unit and the original cost of equipment up to Rs 1 million, if it is a service enterprise. It is this segment that craves the most for funds from the banking sector, as these enterprises do not have access to any other way of funding. Similar is the position of small enterprises, which, in the case of a manufacturing or service enterprise, have an original investment in plant and machinery or equipment used, up to Rs 50 million and 10 million respectively. The government of India is now thinking of changing this definition by basing it on the turnover of a unit rather than on original investment in plant and machinery. The new definition, when adopted, would be more objective and in line with the definition of SMEs in several other countries.

As per the fourth census of MSMEs in the country conducted in 2007-08, as many as 46 per cent of MSME units are located in the rural sector[18]. As stated earlier, only 5.3 per cent of the enterprises in the MSME sector access institutional finance of any form. Being inherently weak, micro and small enterprises stand in need of support and the government does provide several support measures to ensure development of this sector. The support could be in the form of reserved items for production by MSMEs, favourable procurement policy for government departments and organisations, priority sector status for loans, with the target for lending to the micro-enterprise sector by commercial banks and regional rural banks, and finally, a structured mechanism for monitoring credit flow to this segment. Units in the MSME sector are known to become sick for various internal as well as external factors affecting their operation, and when this situation arises, the government expects them to quickly identify their viability, and if found viable, to promptly nurse them back to health with appropriate measures.

The policy atmosphere has been very conducive for providing financial assistance to the MSME sector enterprises, whether it is directly by banks to units identified by them or through various schemes and programmes initiated and sponsored by the government. Banks generally have more freedom in setting lending norms, including interest rates, unlike in the case of agriculture; and when the loan turns non-performing, they have recourse to the Securitisation and Reconstruction of Financial Assets and Enforcement of Security Interests (SARFAESI) Act, in terms of which banks have the power to seize and dispose of the assets without reference to the courts. However, several industry bodies have been complaining that the only sector where the SARFAESI Act provisions are rigorously used is the small enterprise sector and that this leads to banks taking a mechanistic view and not making any support available when the industrial unit is in trouble.

In spite of the conducive policy and several general and segment-specific measures put in place by the government and financial institutions, the common complaint from the sector is that adequate and timely finance is not provided and that in the case of sickness, appropriate support is not extended, causing unnecessary harassment to entrepreneurs. The issues are often discussed in several forums set up for the purpose, including the SLBC, the State Level Empowered Committee of the RBI, and the State Level Inter-Institutional Committee (SLIIC), where both the RBI and state governments have the lead role. However, if the proceedings of these forums are any indication, it seems all is not well with financing of the sector. The same issues go on getting repeated in the agenda of these meetings year after year, hardly any solution to the vexing question of industrial sickness, which occurs due to external factors beyond the control of the units, is arrived at in such forums.

In a unique experiment of its kind, the Government of Telangana has set up a Non-Banking Financial Company (NBFC), the Telangana Industrial Health Clinic Ltd. (TIHCL), with the objective of resolving and preventing sickness and incipient sickness in the manufacturing Micro and Small Enterprises (MSE) sector in the state. It is modelled on a participatory equity stakeholding pattern across the state government, the Government of India, banks and financial institutions, entrepreneurs and other investors and aims at revival, restructuring and rehabilitation of MSEs. The successful performance of the Clinic in meeting its objectives would certainly lead to similar innovations in other states.

The Banking Codes and Standards Board of India (BCSBI), together with the Indian Banks Association (IBA), has put in place a code of conduct for banks financing the MSME sector. The code is available on the website of all member banks. While the customer needs to be aware of these provisions and guidelines, here the industry-level organisations can play a much greater role. On the other side, bank officials also need to continuously update themselves, improve their knowledge, skill and attitude in delivering appropriate products and services to this sector. The capability of the banking sector must be continuously developed to address the financial needs of the sector, the profile of which is also changing fast with the development of technology and changing consumer needs.

Apart from timely and adequate credit, MSEs need to be promptly paid for the products and services they provide. More often than not, this does not happen, especially if the buyer is a large organisation, including a government agency or department. This affects the cash flow of the micro or small enterprise and its viability ultimately comes to be questioned. This has been the cause of sickness in quite a few enterprises. To address the issue of timely payment, the law, the Micro, Small and Medium Enterprises Development Act, 2006 has a provision that the affected enterprise can approach the MSE Facilitation Council set up by the state government. Facilitation Councils are in operation in the states and they do address these issues which are brought to their notice. All said and done, however, this is a case of unequal relationship and a small enterprise would not generally risk its relationship with a larger one if the dues are not paid once or twice as per the purchase terms. Like many other things, marketing is also not easy for small entrepreneurs.

To facilitate generation of cash flow to the seller enterprise, the RBI has formulated the policy of establishing Trade Receivables Discounting System (TReDS), a platform for electronically trading the receivables of a micro or small enterprise. Three institutions have been licensed so far to provide this facility. Both buyers and sellers have to be registered on the platform, where the seller is required to upload the invoice, which will be accepted by the buyer, following which financial institutions, including factoring companies, will bid for the same. Through this process, the seller enterprise would get paid by the intermediary institution which would collect the dues from the buyer at the scheduled time. Although this work was earlier done by the factoring institutions, TReDS is a significant improvement, as it provides an online platform and a transparent way of bidding. How it develops needs to be seen[19].

The loans in respect of MSEs are covered under a Credit Guarantee Scheme (CGS) administered by the Credit Guarantee Trust for Micro and Small Enterprises (CGTMSE), owned by the Government of India and SIDBI. The main requirement for such coverage is that the loan must be without any collateral security or third party guarantee. Loans up to Rs 2 crore are now covered under the CGTMSE guarantee, with the guaranteed sum ranging from 85 per cent to 50 per cent, depending on the loan size and the location as well as the entrepreneur type. This was the only credit guarantee scheme put in place after the Deposit Insurance and Credit Guarantee Corporation (DICGC) discontinued the credit guarantee scheme. It gave an opportunity to banks to finance MSEs without any collateral. However, the scheme has generally suffered because of lack of awareness, both on the part of borrowers and bankers and performance under the scheme has not been up to the mark in spite of regular monitoring at various levels.

The Micro Units Development and Regulatory Agency (MUDRA), set up under the Pradhan Mantri Mudra Yojana (PMMY) in 2015, has re-emphasised credit flow to the micro enterprise sector. MUDRA, which is a Non-Banking Finance Company (NBFC) registered with the RBI, has been providing refinance and other support to banks as well as NBFCs for extending financial assistance to micro enterprises, divided into three segments: Sishu loans up to Rs 50,000, Kishore loans up to Rs 5 lakh, and Tarun loans up to Rs 10 lakh. This focused approach to micro enterprise finance has led to sanction of Rs 4.6 lakh crore in credit from 10.38 crore MUDRA loans; 76 per cent of these accounts are held by women, and more than 50 per cent belong to Scheduled Castes, Scheduled Tribes and Other Backward Classes. The government has set a target for the year 2018-19 for lending by banks and NBFCs under the MUDRA scheme. Needless to add, in earlier years also banks had achieved the target set by the government for the purpose.

Financial Inclusion

Increasingly, robust empirical evidence demonstrates how appropriate financial services can help to improve household welfare and spur small enterprise activity. Macro evidence also shows that economies with deeper financial intermediation and better access to financial services grow faster and have less income inequality. Policy makers and regulators worldwide recognise these connections. They have made financial inclusion where everyone has the choice to access and use the financial services they need, delivered in a responsible fashion, a global development priority.

Financial inclusion means that individuals and enterprises have access to useful and affordable financial products and services that meet their needs – transactions, payment services, savings, credit, and insurance – delivered in a responsible and sustainable way. Access to a transaction account is the first step towards broader financial inclusion, since it allows people to store money, send and receive payments. A transaction account can serve as a gateway to various financial services, which is why we have seen in the earlier chapters details of the steps taken by the RBI and the government and the pressure put on the banking system in India to open small accounts in the names of individuals who stood excluded from the formal banking system.

Rapid economic growth in India in the recent past has brought in its wake a number of concerns, which relate to expanding this growth across regions, sectors, and people. The major objective is to ensure inclusive growth by removing the constraints of poor infrastructure, improving economic efficiency and spreading the benefits of growth over a vast population, which has remained outside the purview of this development process. The financial sector in the country has also experienced revolutionary changes but there exists a large number of people for whom the financial services revolution has effectively passed by, resulting in financial exclusion of this segment. Financial exclusion, which is generally the outcome of poverty, ignorance and environmental factors, is to a great extent related to supply side issues, i.e. lack of appropriate financial services for those that are excluded by the traditional system of instruments.

Keeping in view the need for the banking system to take urgent steps to bring about financial inclusion in the country, the RBI, in the mid-term review of the Annual Policy for 2005-06, exhorted banks to make available a basic banking 'no frills' account either with nil or very low balances as well as charges that would make such accounts accessible to vast sections of the population. The nature and number of transactions in such accounts would be restricted and would be made known to customers in advance in a transparent manner. Soon after this, in January 2006, the RBI came out with guidelines for appointment of BFs and BCs, about which we have already discussed in earlier chapters. Several banks, both in the public and private sectors, have responded positively to this measure and devised no-frills accounts for the lower income groups. The Pradhan Mantri Jan Dhan Yojana (PMJDY), which has been discussed earlier in this book, took financial inclusion in the country forward in a way not seen before and ended up by opening 180 million basic accounts, small accounts as defined under the PML Act in a span of just about one year, between August 2014 and August 2015.

Although such basic bank accounts are generally considered unprofitable, in view of low balances and a large number of transactions which are expensive for banks to maintain, the provision of such deposit accounts has been accepted the world over as a stepping stone to financial inclusion. In a somewhat different way, this requires bank branches to be aware of the surrounding areas in which they work and promote a more outward-looking, customer-centric model to work alongside their usual profit-driven model. A basic no frills account is just the beginning of a relationship and can pave the way to the customer availing a variety of savings products and loan products for consumption, housing, etc. The account can be used for sanctioning small overdraft facilities and making small-value remittances at low cost. The same banking account can also be used by state governments to provide social security services like health and calamity insurance under various schemes for the disadvantaged. Having such social security cover makes the financing of such persons less risky from the bank's point of view and they can be financed for various purposes. Further, holders of no-frills accounts who would be beneficiaries of the Employment Guarantee Scheme (EGS) of the Government of India can also be customers of banks over a longer time horizon.

It is almost a cliché that rural credit should adhere to the basic requirements of timeliness, adequacy and hassle-free delivery, apart from taking care of the financial needs of the customer in a holistic manner, including consumption credit. To address these issues, several credit card schemes have been devised and implemented by banks in the past. Such schemes have the flexibility of use and they fulfil the above requirements to a substantial extent. But all these schemes have so far been activity-specific, i.e. for farmers, artisans, etc. Under financial inclusion, however, the need was felt for an all-purpose credit card for the first-time entrants into the banking system. The General Credit Card (GCC) did not target any specific functional group but had the potential to address the credit needs of persons with small means having some income-generating activity, without bothering so much about the nature of the activity. The scheme was revised in 2013 allowing banks to issue GCCs for any amount as long as the loan was for the purpose of non-farm entrepreneurial activity and was otherwise eligible for classification as the priority sector loan. The card limit was required to be fixed on the basis of risk assessment on a case-to-case basis.

For the financial sector, the mode of delivery of services is as important as the nature of services to be delivered, as it has several implications for financial institutions. It is generally agreed that any delivery of financial services should take into account the issues associated with (i) outreach, (ii) impact and (iii) sustainability of the programme. This matrix was developed in the context of microfinance but is valid for financial inclusion too. To be considered successful, a programme must have extensive outreach to cover a large number of targeted people, must have an impact on the way they conduct their life and in the process must be sustainable. It is nobody's case that a financial institution would incur losses in trying to reach out to the rural and financially excluded population.

The BC system, which provided the much needed innovation on the delivery mechanism for facilitating financial inclusion, also suffered from policy confusion, as we have already discussed in Chapter 2. When the policy was first announced in January 2006, certain types of institutions and individuals were made eligible to be BCs of banks, as it was thought prudent to restrict the number and nature of these entities in view of the fact that they were supposed to deal with cash on behalf of banks and due diligence was required to be done even in eligible cases. Subsequently, however, the universe of eligible institutions and individuals that could be appointed as BCs was expanded and the manner in which BCs were appointed was also modified from time to time. BCs were required to provide doorstep banking services in villages and this had to be done with the help of technology. The BC carried a hand-held device with which transactions could be done either with smart cards issued to customers or with the help of mobile phones, depending on which technology was adopted by the bank. Since banks did not have the technology in house, they went in for outsourcing and technology service providers (TSPs) became an important partner in the financial inclusion process. Some of them also helped banks in the appointment of BCs. That is how we came to have BCs appointed by banks themselves co-existing with BCs appointed by TSPs, which were known as corporate BCs. Over a period of time, several banks started depending on TSPs for this purpose and a situation arose, in which the person who was to represent the bank in the village was actually appointed by someone else, with banks developing an attitude of indifference towards the BC. Banks' ownership of BCs suffered in the process, leading to perfunctory training imparted to them and haphazard implementation of the BC scheme.

With all its good intentions, the Government of India also contributed to the confusion. In 2011-12, the Department of Financial Services of the Ministry of Finance started issuing instructions to banks on the manner of appointment of BCs. A view was taken by the department that banks should appoint BCs on a zonal basis, with one company selected by a bank to act as corporate BC in a zone. The work done by banks thus far had to be annulled and bidding started afresh, throwing the whole system in disarray. There was utter confusion at the ground level and nobody was sure as to what the next step would be. Sometimes, the guidelines of the Ministry clashed with those issued by the RBI, as in the case of Ultra Small Branches (USB) (the RBI's definition of USB was different from the Ministry's definition, creating avoidable confusion at the operational level) and to the discomfiture of the RBI, the Ministry started issuing instructions to public sector banks in matters of opening branches and setting up ATMs in rural and semi-urban centres. The confusion ended when the guidelines for appointment of zone-wise corporate BCs was put in cold storage and not followed up by the Government. But by that time, enough damage had been done to the system which was now fighting for credibility. Banks slowly reverted to the earlier system of appointing TSPs and BCs. Even then there was a fear that with such a large number of BCs on the ground doing work similar to banking as done at bank branches, they could be a potential threat to the system, as they could at a later date, unionise and claim parity with banks in matters of service conditions. The experience with RRBs was too fresh in the mind of banks. So long as this does not happen, banks are happy to use BCs as their extended arms to provide financial services in the rural sector to the persons hitherto excluded from the banking system.

A report by Microsave on the State of Agency Network (SAN) in India in 2017 shows that BCs reported 'lack of resources to buy enough cash or e-money, frequent service downtime, and poor Internet connectivity as the top three barriers to doing agency banking business in the country'[20]. In the previous year, the report had shown the lack of awareness of services among customers as the top-most barrier. Presumably, this factor has been taken care of by concerted action by service providers to increase awareness among the users of banks' services. Nevertheless, connectivity issues still remain a major hindrance in rural areas, as BCs would be able to perform well only if the infrastructure is available. Added to this is the lack of proper monitoring and close liaison with BCs and bank branches. It is no wonder BCs are not able to function to the best of their ability. The same report also states that about 22 per cent of BCs in India faced frauds during the year, which was a significant jump from only 2 per cent reported a year ago. It also elaborates that the incidence of fraud is higher (29 per cent) among high-performing agents (defined as those with above 40 transactions a day), probably because they conduct more number of transactions.

To enable banks to monitor BCs effectively, setting up USBs by banks in rural areas was allowed. These are intermediate structures between the base branch to which the BC is attached and the place where the BC operates. The distance between the base branch and the place where the BC operates, stipulated earlier (30 km in rural areas and 5 km in urban/metropolitan areas) has been done away with by the RBI and it is now incumbent on banks to ensure proper oversight of BCs working on its behalf and accordingly frame a board-approved policy. According to the RBI guidelines, BCs can operate from USBs, as their association with a bank branch would give them credibility and give confidence to people in dealing with them. However, since BCs have been envisaged as agents who would provide doorstep banking, they have to be mobile and not fixed to any branch. The RBI has also acknowledged this in the same guidelines.

There is an urgent need for banks to take ownership of BCs, train them appropriately and at regular intervals and show them as part of the extended banking system, so that people can develop confidence in them and trust them with their money. At present, training of BCs in many cases is undertaken by TSPs and in some cases, imparted by banks but the duration and coverage of such training programmes is not adequate to truly build their capacity to effectively act as representatives of mainstream banks. With the emergence of Payments Banks on the scene, which can also act as BCs of mainstream banks, the financial inclusion scene is poised for more action and the onus will increasingly be on banks to develop an appropriate framework for continuous monitoring as well as supporting of BCs.

In fact, there is a need for banks to redesign their business strategies to incorporate specific plans to promote financial inclusion of low-income groups treating it not only as a corporate social responsibility but also as a business opportunity. The business opportunity lies in exploiting the low margins-high volumes situation at the 'bottom of the pyramid' and seen in this context, financial inclusion would not only be socially desirable but would also make a lot of economic sense. To quote noted economist Professor C. H. Hanumantha Rao, "Considering the prevailing socio-economic structure and the nature of our polity, the challenges for achieving more inclusive growth are much greater than for stepping up the GDP growth rate." Financial inclusion opens the possibilities of other types of inclusion and coupled with appropriate policies, it has the potential to lead to overall inclusive growth of the society.

Government-sponsored Schemes

The government has promoted several rural and urban development programmes to eradicate poverty. These programmes basically aim at either poverty reduction or employment generation or both. Quite a few of these programmes involve bank loans, the remaining being funded by the government directly. The integrated Rural Development Programme (IRDP) was once the biggest attack on poverty in rural areas and involved bank credit for generation of low-value assets which could improve the beneficiary's income and improve his standard of living. It reached about 50 million beneficiaries since its inception in 1980. However, a government evaluation showed that only about 15 per cent beneficiaries could cross the poverty line. Another study showed that 24 per cent of assets did not generate any income, and 50 per cent of assets did not make any contribution to the net disposable income[21].

The scope of poverty reduction through the IRDP was limited both by the debt-capacity of the poor and by the high cost of appraising, monitoring and enforcing small loan agreements. The first limitation was in theory offset by government subsidy but it attracted rich borrowers too to the scheme and thus created political and administrative problems. The subsidy element led to large-scale corruption on the part of lower level functionaries, who certified beneficiaries as being below the poverty line. It also led to corruption on the part of bank staff and on the part of borrowers themselves, some of whom sold off their assets and pocketed the subsidy or who borrowed by proxy for non-target group borrowers. Thus, a scheme which had the potential of bringing about direct poverty reduction in rural areas ended in controversy. The IRDP was generally successful in places where infrastructural and institutional support was readily available. However, these are the very places where even without government subsidy, economic activities can be undertaken by people and can help in lifting their living standards. It was unsuccessful in several places because the support and linkages were not available. Further, provision of credit was taken as a one-time event that would alter the life of the borrower. The fact that multiple doses of credit may be necessary and that it needs to be accompanied by other facilitating developments to ensure proper end use was not considered. The whole programme seemed to be driven by available funds for subsidy rather than any potential-based demand for credit. The failure of the IRDP compelled the government to take cognizance of these factors in subsequent programmes.

The Swarnjayanti Gram Swarojgar Yojana (SGSY) was launched in 1999, replacing the IRDP and a few other programmes, to bring the assisted poor families above the poverty line, by organising them into SHGs through the process of social mobilisation, their training and capacity building and provision of income generating assets through a mix of bank credit and government subsidy. The scheme emphasised the establishment of activity clusters through selection of key activities based on aptitude and skill of people, availability of resources and market opportunity. The scheme adopted a process approach and attempted to build the capacities of the rural poor. It provided for involvement of NGOs/banks and Self-Help Promoting Institutions (SHPIs) in nurturing and development of SHGs, including skill development. The focus of the programme was on establishing a large number of micro enterprises in rural areas, based on the ability of the poor and the potential of each area for sustainable income generation. It took care of several weaknesses found in the case of the IRDP but gave rise to some other issues, which were soon observed during the implementation process.

Since its inception, the SGSY assisted in the formation of 35.7 lakh SHGs, and assisted 1.24 crore SHG members (called Swarozgaris) in establishing their own micro enterprises. The Government of India released Rs 11,486 crore under the programme, with bank credit mobilisation at Rs 19,017 crore. A study showed that it failed to take off in many cases, could not mobilise the credit as per targets, did not succeed in its attempt to target the real poor and vulnerable sections and resulted in low survival rate of promoted micro enterprises and low, less than anticipated realised additional income from micro enterprises[22]. Banks were not wholeheartedly participating in the programme due to high NPAs and there were pilferages at different stages of implementation of the programme. The government wanted to re-design the programme to get rid of its serious limitations.

The National Rural Livelihoods Mission (NRLM), also called Aajeevika, was launched by the Ministry of Rural Development, Government of India, in June 2011. Aided in part through investment support by the World Bank, the Mission aimed at creating efficient and effective institutional platforms for the rural poor, enabling them to increase household income through sustainable livelihood enhancements and improved access to financial services. It replaced the SGSY and set out with an agenda to cover 7 crore rural poor households, across 600 districts, 6000 blocks, 2.5 lakh Gram Panchayats and 6 lakh villages in the country, through self-managed SHGs and federated institutions and support them for livelihood collectives in a period of 8-10 years. This is the programme that is currently in operation. The NRLM is a highly process-oriented programme and requires intensive application of resources, both financial and human, in order to mobilise the poor into functionally effective institutions, promote their financial inclusion and diversify and strengthen their livelihoods. It was, therefore, not feasible to roll out the programme in full scale across the country in one go and, therefore, it was decided to phase the programme implementation over a period of 10 years.

In addition, the poor would be facilitated to achieve increased access to rights, entitlements and public services, diversified risk and better social indicators of empowerment. The NRLM, subsequently named Deendayal Antyoday Yojana, believes in harnessing the innate capabilities of the poor and complements them with capacities (information, knowledge, skills, tools, finance and collectivisation) to participate in the growing economy of the country. A huge superstructure has since been built to implement the programme with the help of state governments and other stakeholders.

All credit-linked schemes, sponsored by the government, involve bank credit as well as government subsidy. While government subsidy is mostly back-ended, i.e. it is paid towards the end of the repayment period for the bank loan, it is the bank credit that faces several challenges. The borrower often confuses between bank loan and government grant. The only way to ensure repayment of loan is to ensure proper utilisation of funds, which can be done only through joint action by banks and the government. But in practice, this is seldom achieved.

Bank loans to SHGs under the NRLM are under an interest subvention scheme. As per the scheme, the loans to SHGs will have to be at 7 per cent per annum and the Government of India would provide subvention at a rate equal to the difference between the weighted average interest charged to SHGs by a bank, and 7 per cent. Thus the actual subvention would vary from bank to bank. An additional subvention of 3 per cent is also given to the SHG which makes prompt repayment of the loan, very much similar to agriculture loans. Some state governments provide additional subvention to SHGs, as in the case of Andhra Pradesh, loans up to Rs 5 lakh to SHGs are actually interest-free. The state government bears the interest on such loans.

A mid-term review in 2017 by the Institute of Rural Management, Anand (IRMA), commissioned by the Ministry of Rural Development, shows progress on several parameters[23]. It has, however, shown that despite some of its noteworthy achievements, the scheme has faced several constraints and challenges. In terms of programme-level issues, the depth and width of outreach across states have not been uniform. Considerable variations have been observed in the implementation of strategies and operations owing to structural and resource constraints. The adoption of target-oriented approach for performance monitoring may also have the effect of diluting the quality of processes in the long run and the emphasis on converging with so many local-level programmes could also result in dilution of the core process agenda. Nevertheless, expectations are high from this programme, as it is one of the most important poverty alleviation programmes implemented so far in the country.

While these programmes were related to poverty alleviation in rural areas and integrated rural development, there were specific programmes focused on employment generation in the case of educated unemployed youth. Unemployment is seen as a major socio-economic problem which has the potential to derail the bogie of economic progress in the country. The small scale industrial sector, which included the village and cottage industrial sector, was, therefore, found to be the best means to solve the growing unemployment problem in the country. Policy makers, who studied and analysed the situation, concluded that by setting up small-scale units with modest investments, employment could be provided to 4 or 5 persons, directly and indirectly. The satisfaction of self-employment and providing employment to a few others could also have a positive multiplier effect. In view of this, employment generation schemes focused on setting up of micro and small enterprises through government subsidy and bank credit and in the process provide employment to the educated people.

The Government of India had launched a scheme called the Self-Employment Scheme for Educated Unemployed Youth (SEEUY) in 1985, under which financial assistance was provided for setting up small industrial and service units. District Industries Centres (DICs) operated this scheme at the district level. However, it could not be continued successfully, as around 70 per cent of the units became sick and closed down. The scheme was later subsumed in the Prime Minister's Rojgar Yojana (PMRY), which came into effect in 1993. The main objective of the PMRY was to provide financial assistance to the educated unemployed youth to set up own enterprises in manufacturing, services and trade-related activities. The scheme operated through fixing annual targets for assistance, state-wise and bank-wise, identification of beneficiaries through Task Force Committees, which comprise developmental agencies as well as banks, providing training to selected candidates, lending by banks and periodical monitoring and reviewing of performance under the scheme at various levels.

The scheme, however, suffered from the usual maladies that a government-sponsored scheme is seen to be associated with, such as interference at the level of selection of beneficiaries, absence of proper appraisal by banks, poor financial discipline of borrowers and lack of adequate supervision and monitoring of project implementation, which led to piling up of non-performing loans in this segment. NPAs sometimes rose to as high as 40 per cent, as a major portion of the units set up became sick. As we repeatedly see in our system, there is pressure on banks to lend. In every forum, shortfall in lending is highlighted and the banks concerned pulled up for not achieving targets with hardly any commensurate discussion anywhere on how loans are utilised and whether loans are repaid in time. We need to discuss the entire credit cycle, not only a part of it because it is politically expedient or because it is convenient for the bureaucrats overseeing implementation of schemes. Generally, it is assumed that the lending banks would take care of the remaining part of the credit cycle. They would monitor end-use of funds and recovery of loans. The realities are different. Banks have a general feeling of being coerced into lending under the schemes and more often than not, appraisal and monitoring are not done properly, as a result of which NPA levels soar. Even the forums under the LBS, such as the Block Level Bankers Committee (BLBC), the District Consultative Committee (DCC) and the State Level Bankers Committee (SLBC), do not generally flag utilisation and recovery issues, as much as they do on lending targets and their achievements. Here and there, some meeting raises the issue, requests the government to provide assistance in recovery but not much happens afterwards. The PMRY also suffered a similar fate.

The Prime Minister's Rural Employment Generation Programme was launched in August 2008, by merging the PMRY with another scheme, which was being operated by the Khadi and Village Industries Commission (KVIC), called the Rural Employment Generation Programme (REGP). The new programme was taken over by the KVIC and operated by it as a credit-linked subsidy programme of the Ministry of Micro, Small and Medium Enterprises (MSME), Government of India. Currently, it is the flagship programme of the Ministry and serves as an instrument for the generation of employment opportunities in urban and rural areas through setting up of micro enterprises.

There are several other programmes being implemented by the Central Government as well as by various state governments. Many of them do not involve bank finance. A common complaint against the schemes involving bank credit is that beneficiaries often mix up credit-linked schemes with those purely funded by the government. Lack of financial literacy, lack of awareness about scheme details and the fact that a significant part of banking sector is in the hands of the government, only helps to reinforce this view. Borrowers who are beneficiaries of such schemes do not think repayment is necessary and regular loan waivers in the agriculture sector provide fodder for this. The result is low level of loan utilisation and high level of NPAs with banks. Another issue is the emphasis placed on self-employment or entrepreneurship development in several of these programmes. As we have seen, major programmes aim at creating micro enterprises and not leading to wage employment. While this is a laudable goal, the psychology of a typical person who is educated and unemployed may not fully support this approach.

Formal education in our country in itself has not been able to make the youth employable. Further training is always required if someone is to be made suitable for a job. Skill development, therefore, is an important parameter in any policy prescription for increasing employment or reducing poverty. Skill development can relate to either setting up a small enterprise, in which case entrepreneurial skill along with other functional skill would be necessary or it can be purely wage-related employment in various sectors and activities. The Government of India urged banks to set up Rural Self Employment Institutes (RSETIs), based on the earlier successful model of Rural Development and Self Employment Institutes (RUDSETIs), set up by Syndicate Bank and Canara Bank in Karnataka and elsewhere in the country. As we have seen earlier, 586 RSETIs have been established. Their settlement record as on March 2018 is over 82 per cent, with 8.4 per cent beneficiaries getting employed on wage basis and the remaining 01.6 per cent taking up some self-employment ventures. Of the latter, a little more than 50 per cent have availed bank finance[24]. The Deen Dayal Upadhyaya Grameen Kaushal Yojana (DDUGKY), which is implemented by the Ministry of Rural Development as a skill-focused programme, shows less than 20 per cent achievement, although the scheme entirely focuses on wage employment and has an elaborate structure and network implementing it.

In spite of several drawbacks associated with government-sponsored schemes involving bank finance, one positive aspect for banks which generally goes unnoticed is that banks get customers on a platter. For acquiring the same number of customers whether in rural or urban areas, banks would have to struggle and compete with one another. The only requirement is to follow the guidelines issued in respect of each scheme, let the bank official get fully involved in the selection of borrowers, do the appraisal as per due norms and monitor the implementation jointly with the local government officials and agencies associated with the scheme. Simultaneously, provision of financial literacy to the intending beneficiaries under the schemes and educating them about the schemes' details would go a long way to make them understand their role vis-a-vis the financing institutions and the government.

Under each of the above programmes, there have been some success stories. There have been stories of people who started with nothing and with the help of bank credit and subsidy succeeded in setting up thriving enterprises. But unfortunately, in an overwhelming majority of cases, funds were never used for the purpose for which these were meant and the schemes, therefore, did not have any impact on the lives of the people who were assisted under them. For want of a better alternative, however, such schemes go on getting announced every year and a lot of money is spent in the process.

Policies relating to rural finance, like any other policy, change over time, taking into account emerging realities as also priorities of the government. The banking sector has seen continuous changes taking place in the recent past, with new ideas being thrown in and old practices getting overthrown. The changes relate to banking laws and practices, regulatory requirements and products and processes through which banking service is provided to customers. Over a period of time, the sector has developed the resilience needed to withstand such changes and has responded to them quite well. New banking and financial terms have been internalised. One factor, which has brought about significant changes in banking and has changed the face of rural banking and made financial inclusion possible, is technology which we shall deal with in the next chapter.

5

Technology – Enabling the Enabler

THE relationship between banking and technology has been quite fascinating. Technology has entered the banking arena in a big way so much so that the profile of a bank today gets defined more by technology than by anything else. Today, we simply cannot imagine banking without technology. It has greatly enhanced the speed and quality of services provided by the banking sector. Not only the overall banking landscape but especially the path to financial inclusion has been impacted by technology, particularly the Information and Communication Technology (ICT). Financial inclusion has always been a policy focus. Although the phrase 'financial inclusion' was coined in the middle of the last decade, the objective to provide banking services to a vast multitude of financially excluded persons, mostly living in rural and less accessible areas, could not be fulfilled for want of appropriate technology. Now we can talk about financial inclusion confidently because we have the technology in place to reach the huge numbers in a cost-effective manner.

Developments in the field of Information Technology (IT) have supported the growth and inclusiveness of the banking sector. Not only has it enhanced the competitive efficiency of the banking sector by strengthening the back-end administrative processes but it has also contributed to the improvement of the front-end system and helped in bringing down transaction costs and improving efficiency for delivery of customer service. And, the service delivery has been greatly enabled in the context of the customers with small means, the high-volume, low-value segment, whose inclusion in the formal financial system is being advocated under the financial inclusion initiative.

A major technological development in the banking sector has been the adoption of Core Banking Solutions (CBS). The CBS is networking of branches, which enables customers to operate their accounts and avail banking services from any branch of the bank on the CBS network, regardless of where the customer maintains his/her account. The customer is no more the customer of a branch, as he becomes the bank's customer. Thus, the CBS is a step towards enhancing customer convenience through anywhere, anytime banking. It is important to leverage on to this technological advancement to look at areas beyond the CBS that can help in not just delivering quality and efficient services to customers but also generating and managing information effectively.

Another major technological development, which has revolutionised the delivery channel in the banking sector, has been the growth of ATMs. The banking space has seen considerable growth through ATMs (approximately 2,06,000 ATMs as on December 2017), covering urban/metro areas as well as semi-urban and rural areas. The RBI has also permitted non-banks to set up, own and operate ATMs to accelerate the growth and penetration of ATMs in the country. Such ATMs, known as White Label ATMs (WLA), provide ATM services to customers of all banks.

With the growth of the economy, both paper-based payments and electronic payments have recorded significant improvement. The RBI had introduced Magnetic Ink Character Recognition (MICR) technology for speeding up and bringing in efficiency in processing of cheques. Recent developments in paper-based instruments include the launch of Speed Clearing (for local clearance of outstation cheques drawn on core banking-enabled branches of banks) and introduction of Cheque Truncation System (CTS) to restrict physical movement of cheques and enable the use of images for payment processing. Use of paper-based instruments such as cheques, drafts, etc., accounted for nearly 11 per cent of the volume of total non-cash retail transactions in the country in 2016-17, a significant reduction from around 26 per cent in 2014-15. In value terms, the share in 2016-17 was around 37 per cent, down from 55 per cent during 2014-15[1]. At present, the policy thrust is to reduce the use of paper for transactions and move towards electronic mode.

Various electronic payment services are available in the country. These include Electronic Clearing Service (ECS)/ National ECS (NECS), which is used by institutions for making bulk payment of amounts towards distribution of dividend, interest, salary, pension, etc., or for bulk collection of amounts towards various dues from people having bank accounts. The National Electronic Funds Transfer (NEFT) is a payment system facilitating one-to-one funds transfer. Under this, individuals, firms and corporates can electronically transfer funds from any bank branch to any individual, firm or corporate having an account with any other bank branch in the country participating in the scheme. Thus, this is an inter-bank fund transfer system. The Real Time Gross Settlement (RTGS) system, on the other hand, is a continuous (real-time) settlement of funds transfer individually on an order-by-order basis (without netting). 'Real Time' means the processing of instructions at the time they are received rather than at some later time, and 'Gross Settlement' signifies that the settlement of funds transfer instruction occurs individually (on an instruction-by-instruction basis). Considering that fund settlement takes place in the books of the RBI, payments are final and irrevocable.

Pre-paid Payment Systems have also been introduced. Pre-Paid Instruments (PPIs) are payment instruments that facilitate purchase of goods and services against the value stored on these instruments.

PPIs are issued in the form of smart cards, magnetic stripe cards, Internet accounts, Internet wallets, mobile accounts, mobile wallets, paper vouchers, etc.

In addition, there are around 30.28 lakh Point of Sale (PoS) terminals in the country (December 2017), which enable customers to make payments for purchase of goods and services by means of credit or debit cards. To facilitate customer convenience, the RBI has also permitted cash withdrawal using debit cards issued by banks at POS terminals.

The adoption of technology in the context of financial inclusion has, however, been path-breaking. As we have seen, financial inclusion in the country had suffered due to several supply side as well as demand side factors. The supply side factors were borne out of the rigidity in the banking system, with set systems and processes, the high cost of transactions and the difficulty to reach out to the last mile. The demand side issues, on the other hand, emerged out of the lack of financial literacy, absence of any regular and dependable cash flow and inability of a person to visit the bank branch again and again for even small-value transactions. Here, clearly technology had a role.

The introduction of BCs in the rural sector as agents of banks for providing financial services at the doorstep of customers gave rise to the deployment of new technology in the field. If banking services were to be made affordable to the masses, it had to be made available at places and times which were convenient to them. Carrying out banking transactions away from bank branches, however, required access to the bank's database from a remote area and ideally, which would enable the conduct of online transactions. Apart from a hand-held machine, this also called for reliable telecommunication networks at the village level. To transform the entire eco-system of public services through the use of IT, the Government of India has launched the Digital India Programme with the vision to transform India into a digitally-empowered society and knowledge economy. Common Service Centres (CSCs), under this programme, are allowed to be BCs of banks and hence they play an important role in financial inclusion in the country.

While there was tremendous pressure on banks to deliver on the financial inclusion front and a time-bound action plan had to be prepared by each bank with the approval of its Board of Directors, it also called for exemplary coordination between banks, the government and telecom agencies so as to ensure connectivity. Complaints were flowing from all parts of the country with regard to non-availability of a reliable communication network and even where VSATs were used, there were problems with the bandwidth and speed. As already mentioned in the previous chapter, a Microsave report on Agency Network in India 2017 has stated that frequent service downtime and poor Internet connectivity were the topmost barriers in doing agency banking in the country.

Technology and Rural Banks

True, the technological developments that were taking place involved commercial banks. RRBs being an important component of the banking system in the country were also required to adopt technology in a time-bound manner. However, this came for them with a time lag. Their sponsor banks had a major responsibility in carrying through the process of technology adoption, starting with the CBS. The RBI wanted all RRBs to come on the CBS platform by September 2011. Many banks did adopt the CBS by that date and the remaining did it subsequently. As of now, all the 56 RRBs in the country are on the CBS and are in a position to offer anywhere anytime banking like commercial banks. Other facilities, such as Internet and mobile banking, are also being extended to them in a phased manner, subject to fulfillment of certain conditions. In November 2015, all RRBs on CBS were allowed to provide non-transactional Internet banking. For providing Internet banking with transactional facility, they were required to comply with certain conditions, which related to their level of capital (capital to risk weighted assets ratio or CRAR), net worth, gross NPA level, profitability and record of regulatory compliance.

Due to policy guidelines issued by the RBI and NABARD and sustained efforts made by the stakeholders, all State Cooperative Banks and a majority of District Central Cooperative Banks are also now on the CBS and are in a position to offer technology-based banking products to their customers. Technology adoption by the PACS, however, is a contentious issue, with significant variation in the level of technology adoption among states. The Union Budget of 2017-18 had made an allocation of Rs 1900 crore over a period of three years for bringing digital banking to the PACS. This was aimed at linking 63,000 PACS with the CBS of DCCBs, allowing new generation banking services to be made available to the small and marginal farmers who are members of these societies.

Since November 2015, State Cooperative Banks and DCCBs (as also Urban Cooperative Banks) having necessary infrastructure are also allowed to provide the Internet banking facility to their customers, subject to fulfilment of certain criteria, similar to RRBs, relating to their capital adequacy, net worth, NPA level, profitability, and record of regulatory compliance.

As per the RBI guidelines, mobile banking has also been extended to RRBs, SCBs, DCCBs and UCBs. Mobile banking, which involves use of a mobile phone for carrying out banking activities, assumes greater significance in the context of financial inclusion. Rapid growth of mobile phone users in India, through wider coverage of mobile networks, has made this an important platform for extending banking services, especially to the unbanked segment of the population.

In fact, functioning in a technologically-enabled environment alongside commercial banks is both a challenge and an opportunity for RRBs and cooperative banks, which now need to leverage more on their core competencies and customer orientation to garner more business as also to provide better customer service.

Aadhaar

Aadhaar is a 12-digit unique number which the Unique Identification Authority of India (UIDAI) has issued to the residents of the country. The authority aims at providing a unique number to all Indians, which is stored in a centralised database and linked to the basic demographics and biometric information – name, sex, address, photograph, ten fingerprints and iris of each individual. The information is easily verifiable in an online, cost-effective way. The system is supposed to be unique and robust enough to eliminate the large number of duplicate and fake identities that existed in Government and private databases.

Aadhaar-based identification had two unique features: the universality that was ensured because Aadhaar was expected to be recognised and accepted over time across the country and across all service providers, and every resident's entitlement to the number. With the introduction of this UID number, verification of customer details for know-your-customer (KYC) procedure by banks had also become easy. As Aadhaar card issued by the UIDAI served as identification of a person as well as her address, this document alone was sufficient to ensure KYC formalities. The e-KYC procedure required the customer of a bank to provide only the Aadhaar number at the time of opening of an account, whereupon the bank would connect to the UIDAI server and download the identification details of the customer. No other document was required for the purpose.

The Government of India had made it mandatory to link all new as well as existing bank accounts with the Aadhaar number of the account holder. Apart from ensuring KYC norms, this would also help in channelising Government benefits into the bank accounts, wherever required. The aim was to ultimately transfer all benefits, subsidies, etc. through these accounts only. A beginning was made in respect of transfer of subsidy to LPG users and in a few other cases too, transfers of benefits were made to the bank accounts of the beneficiaries, thereby eliminating the use of physical delivery of cheques or cash to them.

The flip side in making all benefit payments linked to Aadhaar was that in the absence of authentication for some reason, the beneficiary would not be able to avail of the facilities. With the type of infrastructure we have in rural areas in many places, particularly inaccessible areas and hilly areas, there have been incidents reported in the Press of people being refused certain facilities, such as commodities from the public distribution system (PDS), as their identity could not be got approved by the Aadhaar database for connectivity related issues. Such a scenario was definitely undesirable and there should have been an alternative in such cases, to ensure that people did not suffer. The problem with Aadhaar was probably that it aimed too big to issue unique IDs to all citizens in a very short time period, with the facilities available in the country and in spite of the constraints that the system suffered from.

The Aadhaar Enabled Payment System (AEPS), which was an initiative taken up by National Payments Corporation of India (NPCI), an umbrella organisation for all retail payment systems in India and started by joint efforts of RBI and Indian Banks' Association (IBA), is a payment service empowering a bank customer to use Aadhaar as her identity to access her respective Aadhaar enabled bank account and perform basic banking transactions like balance enquiry, cash deposit, cash withdrawal and remittances through a Business Correspondent (BC), a bank representative. The AEPS system leverages Aadhaar online authentication and enables Aadhaar enabled bank accounts to be operated in anytime-anywhere banking mode through micro ATMs. A micro ATM is a biometric authentication enabled hand-held device (also known as a Point of Transaction or PoT terminal), which serves as the doorstep banking system and is generally carried by a BC when she goes to the doorstep of the customers to transact some business involving deposit or withdrawal of cash. The beneficiary bearing a UID number approaches a BC with the request to withdraw cash. The BC feeds the beneficiary's UID number, fingerprints and amount into the micro-ATM. A micro-ATM can perform all types of transactions including deposits and transfers. The Aadhaar server authenticates the beneficiary's ID and gets his bank account using the ID mapper. Once this is successful, the debit and credit transaction is carried out and then a message is sent to the beneficiary and BC and the beneficiary gets his cash.

Of course, there have been issues with the Aadhaar system, both on the inclusion (numbers issued in bogus names) and the exclusion front (genuine people being denied services for want of Aadhaar or for defects encountered during the authentication process); and there are fears of misuse of personal data stored in the Aadhaar database and used by the Government and other agencies for various purposes. The recent Supreme Court judgement in September 2018 which went into the entire gamut of issues connected with Aadhaar, has, however, restricted the use of Aadhaar for establishing the identity of an individual for any purpose by striking down Section 57 of the Aadhaar Act which allowed private companies to avail Aadhaar data. Hence, Aadhaar data is no more needed for opening of bank accounts. The Court has however emphasized the uniqueness of the Aadhaar number, and has stated that Aadhaar is necessary for availing welfare schemes by the Government.

DBT and the JAM Trinity

The Government of India, after ensuring opening of bank accounts through the PMJDY and issuing unique identity in the form of Aadhaar number, has thought of linking the Jan Dhan account, Aadhaar number and the mobile phone number and named it as JAM Trinity for direct delivery of subsidies and other government benefits to beneficiaries. A combination of the three provides a powerful means for ensuring leakage-proof delivery of services and in the days to come, it will assume greater importance as more and more services are passed through this mechanism.

Direct Benefits Transfer (DBT) to the bank accounts of beneficiaries by government departments has been a major goal of the government, both Central and State. There have been intense discussions about this and many thinkers and opinion leaders have argued that the DBT is the answer to the problems faced by the leakage-prone public service delivery system in the country and the most effective alternative to corruption at various intermediary levels in the delivery system. The government has accepted this line of thinking and one major objective of the thrust on financial inclusion and opening of bank accounts for all is to facilitate the direct transfer of benefits and subsidies from the government to people.

It would be noteworthy in this context to recall the experience of the Government of Andhra Pradesh (undivided), which was the first in the country to start the DBT process in 2008. This was pursuant to the report of a committee set up by the RBI [Committee on Suggesting a Framework for Electronic Benefit Transfer (EBT), Chairman: Dr R. B. Barman], which had in April 2008, recommended a 'one district one bank' model for the EBT, which meant that in a certain district, one bank would take the responsibility of the EBT by the state government. The AP Government rolled out a scheme with commercial banks, some public sector banks and also private sector banks, being allotted districts in which they took the initiative to open accounts and to pass on certain government benefits such as old age pension, students' scholarship and payments under the National Rural Employment Guarantee Act (NREGA). Banks appointed BCs, opened accounts of intended beneficiaries, issued them smart cards and transferred the money when received from the government to these accounts. It came to be known as the AP Smart Card Project. The RBI Committee advocated upscaling of the project and a few other states also adopted a similar method of EBT.[2]

The system worked fine for some time. But at the same time, guidelines had been issued to banks for furthering financial inclusion and as part of that, the RBI directed all LBs in the districts and SLBC Convener Banks at the state level to take active part in preparing and implementing financial inclusion plans (FIPs) at the district and state levels. The Service Area model was generally followed in this and LBs at the district level as well as other banks at the Service Area level started appointing BCs and opening accounts, and these BCs in turn took steps to provide banking services in the villages allotted to the banks under the FIP.

In six districts of AP and elsewhere, where the one district 'one bank' model of the EBT had already been implemented, this came in direct conflict with the operations of the nodal bank for the EBT, which in most cases happened to be different from the LB in the district and other banks to which villages were allotted under the FIP. This led to a situation where BCs of two banks were operating in the same village, one dealing only the with EBT and the other with general banking activities. The situation was not viable for either. Ideally, only one BC should be doing the banking work in a village, including the EBT. At the district level too, the LB was at a disadvantage, as government funds meant for the EBT were not channelised through it. The nodal bank under the DBT did not have any LB responsibility either and mostly did not bother to even participate in regular district level meetings under the LBS, called to review the performance of banks in lending to the priority sector and lending under various government-sponsored schemes. The LB and the SLBC Convener Bank expected government funds to flow through them in recognition of their role in providing development finance in the district. It led to a situation in some districts where it so happened that the state government bade goodbye to the EBT and reverted to the older non-bank system of issuing payments to beneficiaries. Miffed by the problem created by some banks, they allotted the job to the post office, which also had accounts of beneficiaries, but which, unlike banks, did not credit the money to the accounts and instead chose to disburse the benefits to beneficiaries by cash. It turned out to be a huge task of cash management for the post office, which it has been trying to discharge to the best of its ability. Cash management issues, however, keep coming up from time to time. It is ironical that the government of a state, which was a pioneer in the country in the electronic benefit transfer, would choose to revert to a non-bank mode of benefits transfer. Ideally, the banking sector, led by the SLBC convener bank, should have been able to sort out the matter, as the problem was internal to the banking system operating in the state; but for some reason, that did not happen[4].

Risk Management

While technology has helped us in managing several risks, it has at the same time created certain risks of its own which have to be managed properly and promptly. This is particularly important, as any laxity in this regard can cost us in terms of money and erode the confidence of people not only in technology but also in banking. With a large number of first-time users of banking services on board who are also forced to make use of technology, this could mean sliding back to the cash-based system. An estimate of this risk can be found in the Microsave report cited above which says that 35 per cent of BCs assisted customers by actually entering their PINs on their behalf while doing transactions at POS machines.

In India, the RBI, together with banks and financial institutions, has been constantly engaged with managing technology risk and ensuring security of the financial system in an inter-connected world. Almost every day, we hear of funds being siphoned off from bank accounts of unsuspecting persons through unauthorised or fraudulent use of credit and debit cards, Internet banking and through other means. As the financial system progresses technologically so do the activities of criminals, who are also highly technologically advanced and no hardware or software system seems to be immune to concerted attacks at penetration by these elements. The more connected we are, the more vigilant we have to be. The Internet, which has ushered in the information age, is also a breeding ground of many criminal activities.

In essence, the Information and Communication Technology (ICT) has emerged as a key driver that has the potential to accelerate economic growth and development. Policy makers sincerely believe that digitisation can help in the sustained development of the rural economy, as it impacts agriculture, trade and industrial activity and, in the process, helps to reshape the rural economy. ICT applications can also be used to bring transparency and accountability in various socio-economic programmes of the government and that is what is being attempted through the JAM Trinity and DBT. But for all this, people must start using the digital mode of transactions.

Demonetisation and Cashless Transactions

In November 2016, the Government of India took a decision to demonetise higher denomination currency notes of Rs 500 and 1000 with the stated objective of curbing black money and counterfeiting of notes. It was by all accounts an unprecedented move which suddenly rendered currency notes of about 86 per cent in value totally useless. India is primarily a cash-based economy and a major part of transactions are done in cash. Further, a major part of India's population, 83.3 crore out of 121 crore, as per the 2011 Census data, lives in rural areas, where agriculture, combined with the informal micro-enterprises and rural service sectors, constitute the major economic activities. Majority of financial transactions are typically of small values and are carried out with cash. What demonetisation did was to suck out this medium of exchange and the day after this announcement, people, especially in rural areas, were left with no option but to go back to some type of barter system to make both ends meet. Demonetisation also severely affected the store value function of currency notes. Suddenly, people who had saved some money and kept it somewhere in the house to meet exigencies, found themselves at the mercy of the government and had to run from pillar to post to get these notes exchanged at banks in accordance with the policy announced by the government, which kept changing from time to time. Those who have passed through this exercise would remember it as an eerie experience; people forced to stand in queues in front of banks for hours, with no guarantee of getting their notes exchanged when their turn came; people standing patiently in front of ATMs to withdraw whatever money was available as per government policy and enduring all the trouble with the only hope that the government through this exercise would be able to eliminate black money in the system. Corruption and black money had destroyed the body fabric of the nation and people were just fed up with government inaction. They were willing to sacrifice their today so that tomorrow would perhaps be better. Such a situation would have been extremely difficult elsewhere, in a developed country, but India is different.

The Prime Minister, in his televised address to the nation in the evening of November 8, 2016, had furnished three reasons for taking such a drastic step: to curb counterfeiting of high denomination notes, to tackle black money holders in the economy and to stop terrorist finance. As time progressed and the Specified Bank Notes (SBNs) kept getting deposited in bank accounts, the focus was quickly shifted to ushering in a cashless economy, subsequently corrected as less-cash economy, by shifting to digital mode of transactions.

It is true that in India, because of the efforts made by the RBI, the National Payments Corporation of India (NPCI) and banks and financial institutions, people were slowly but steadily shifting to the digital mode of transactions even before demonetisation, as they were getting used to debit and credit cards, Internet banking and mobile banking. The NPCI data shows that the total volume of electronic payments improved from 166.94 million in 2003-04 to 1159.84 million in 2011-12[4]. Banks, at least some of them, were aggressively marketing digital financial products and services and positioning themselves as digital-friendly institutions to attract the young and educated new generation customers. Even in rural areas, thanks to BCs and financial inclusion efforts, banking transactions were being increasingly done digitally. What could have been a natural development now became a forced imposition on the people and in the absence of cash, they were compelled to resort to digital payments with the help of credit or debit cards and Internet banking. Mobile apps were forced upon users who had little other option left.

There is nothing wrong with transition to the digital mode of payments. Many countries have been striving towards that. Digitalisation would lead to formalisation of transactions and would leave behind electronic trails. On the other hand, cash transactions, although more convenient, promoted anonymity. But there was nothing wrong with cash either. It was a time-tested method and its legitimacy derived from the confidence people had on the sovereign guarantee or guarantee of the Central Bank. Not only did cash provide anonymity to transactions, it is also reported to help having better control over one's finances. In several developed countries, such as Germany and Japan, cash still continues to be the preferred mode of payment. Reports show that in Germany, cash is still king and around 53 per cent of retail payments are in cash. The currency to GDP ratio in Japan (in 2015) was 18 per cent, compared to 12.25 per cent in India.

The typical response to demonetisation in India in November 2016 has been that it was a good policy decision but implemented badly. It presumed that there were better ways of dealing with the ground level situation once the decision to demonetise Rs 1000 and Rs 500 currency notes was suddenly announced or at least better ways of implementing the decision should have been found. While this may be correct and there is actually no upper limit to efficiency, one must bear in mind the magnitude and complexity of the logistics required for currency management in a country like India. With over 6 lakh villages, 1.5 lakh bank branches, 4,000 currency chests spread over the length and breadth of the country and with four note presses supplying notes, mainly through 26 RBI offices, it was never an easy task even in normal times. Add to this the element of secrecy which would have prevented any building up of stock of new notes at the currency chests or even at the presses prior to the announcement made by the Prime Minister, and we have a scenario that presented itself as a terrible management challenge. Nobody who had an idea of the mammoth logistical requirements would have expected such a far-reaching decision affecting every citizen of the country to be implemented without any trouble. Movement of currency from one place to another requires coordination among several agencies and moving large amounts of currency at a very short notice itself was a huge problem. Banks too had to manage the transition to new currency notes in addition to their normal duties and the extra effort put in by bank officials at that time has been well documented. ATMs too had to be re-calibrated quickly to accommodate the new notes, which had a different size. In that sense, subject to the constraints that the system faced, perhaps the Central Bank as well as the banking system did a great job. They certainly do not deserve the criticism that they failed to implement the decision properly or that they could not plan things in advance. At the same time, it is not clear why the government chose to introduce Rs 2000 denomination currency notes, while demonetising Rs 1000 denomination notes and why in the initial days, only Rs 2000 denomination notes were printed and supplied to banks instead of Rs 500 and Rs 100 notes, which would have eased the woes of the public to a great extent. Some better planning on this account would have helped. And of course, as in every other system, in banks also, some unscrupulous persons did try to take advantage of the situation by colluding with dishonest customers but this could be managed within the framework of the existing rules. There was hardly any cause for panic on that account. There were even reports of small accounts opened under the PMJDY being used to deposit large sums of cash but as reported, such cases were confined to some accounts only.

The other opinion held and expressed by many in the country, including some senior economists, is that demonetisation though caused short term pain, would lead to long-term gains for the country. Long-term gains would in essence relate to formalisation of the economy, steps towards elimination of black money and digitisation of transactions. If these laudable objectives are achieved, the country can to some extent justify the acute pain that people have undergone due to demonetisation but then no one is actually sure. As in many other cases, it is mainly wishful thinking, dealing as we are with a highly complex society with a complex system of governance. We cannot simply extrapolate the present into the future.

While the jury is still out on whether these objectives have been achieved and, if so, to what extent, and whether at all such a measure, which almost crippled the informal cash-driven economy, including agriculture, was necessary or was there any better policy alternative, one major fallout has been the sharp increase in digital transactions initially forced upon a reluctant and confused population by non-availability of cash and later by government policy. Every month, the RBI has been publishing details of electronic payment systems used during the month, showing both volume and value of the transactions. Data shows that the volume of electronic transactions using all modes rose from 671.5 million in November 2016 to 998.5 million in November 2017 and further to 1064.2 million in December 2017. The value of electronic transactions also rose from Rs 94,004 billion in November 2016 to Rs 1,25,531 billion in December 2017. In this, the highest growth was in respect of the UPI (United Payments Interface), the volume of which increased from 0.3 million to 145.5 million in the same period[5].

We must, however, remember that technology is just an enabler and it is up to the user of technology how and in what manner she would use it. Like other financial services, this would also depend on availability, accessibility and affordability of the product and service, as also the awareness level of the user. Going by the experience till date, it is clear that as far as technology is concerned, we are on the right path but as always, a lot more ground has to be covered.

6

The Road Ahead

THE all-India Inclusix Index, developed by CRISIL to measure financial inclusion at the geographical level, based on four parameters, viz., branch penetration, deposit penetration, credit penetration and insurance penetration, moved up to 58.0 in March 2016 from 50.1 in March 2013. Without taking insurance into account, the score would have been 62.2, which shows a significant improvement in the provision of banking services in the country[1]. Much of it has been attributed to the successful implementation of the PMJDY. However, with only 196 million loan accounts, both with banks (162 million) and MFIs (34 million), as against 1.64 billion deposit accounts, comprehensive financial services have yet to reach a large population at the national level. Further, the number of life insurance policies at 340 million is also much lower than the deposit accounts with banks, indicating a significant gap, which remains to be covered. The Inclusix scores of different states show regional imbalances, with the southern states consistently remaining at the top.

Attention to these details and focusing on the hitherto neglected areas would most likely continue to define the thrust of policy on financial inclusion in the immediate future.

With the first phase of financial inclusion, where the focus was on opening of accounts and providing access to the formal banking system getting over, the focus has shifted to making the large number of bank accounts operational and making the BC system robust so as to effectively reach the last mile. There are also a host of related activities which would have to be simultaneously taken care of. As has happened in the past, both the supply as well as the demand sides would undergo significant changes. With the experience gained in the provision of rural finance, both the policy priorities and the modalities of implementation would have to be re-written. While all the details cannot be foreseen at this stage, certain fundamental aspects of the process would continue to guide the developments.

To quote a report by the Consultative Group to Assist the Poor (CGAP): "As we are projecting ourselves into the future, it is obvious that poor people's lives will continue to change. Financial services have a clear role in helping poor people adapt through these changes to seize opportunities, protect assets, create new livelihoods, cope and mitigate risks, build resilience, and plan for the future. Yet today, there is still a disconnect between the supply of financial services and poor people's financial needs"[2]. The report goes on to add that organisations that are focusing on financial inclusion must ensure that financial services enable poor people's inclusion by improving people's well-being, ensuring better supporting livelihoods, adapting to change and building resilience.

Livelihood at the Policy Focus

We have discussed earlier in the book that the financial sector alone cannot ensure development. It must help the real sector create livelihood opportunities for the poor. While developments in the real sector and the financial sector must go hand-in-hand and reinforce each other, livelihood creation would constitute the focus of any financial services activity in future aimed at the poorer sections of the society. Livelihood generation and maintenance must be the aim of any intervention by any agency, government or otherwise, for improving the well-being of people. We have already seen steps being taken in this direction and in future, these efforts are certainly expected to multiply.

In India, creating employment opportunities for the youth is among the top-most priorities of the government today. We take pride in the fact that India is a young country. More than 50 per cent of India's population is below the age of 25 and more than 65 per cent of the population below the age of 35 years. It is expected that in 2020, the average age of Indians would be 29 years compared to 37 years in China and 48 years in Japan. However, unless the young generation is actually engaged in fruitful economic activities, which would not only keep them busy but also help in creating wealth for the country, the much discussed demographic dividend would actually become a demographic disaster. Promotion of self-employment among the youth by creating opportunities through focused government intervention as also expanding the elbow room for wage employment, which happens when the economy in general grows, leading to growth in certain sectors of the economy, will continue to define the major thrust of policy in future. The government is already moving in this direction by emphasising education, infrastructure and skill development and has announced and implemented several dedicated schemes, such as the setting up of the Rural Self-Employment Training Institutes (RSETIs) by banks, implementation of the Deen Dayal Upadhyay Grameen Kaushal Yojana (DDU-GKY) by the Ministry of Rural Development, establishment of Pradhan Mantri Kaushal Kendras at the district level, etc., in addition to the existing vocational training infrastructure. These focused programmes supplement employment generation in sectors such as micro and small enterprises as well as the services sector. In the days to come, creation of jobs and promotion of entrepreneurship in rural areas as much as in urban areas is going to be of utmost importance. The major focus of financial services and micro enterprise development in the rural sector would be to make this happen.

As the rural society keeps changing, the new rural finance paradigm would be based on the premise that 'rural people are bankable'. The rural clientele would not be limited only to farmers and the uneducated or not-so-well-educated but would also include a generation which can use and adopt technology in its evolving form. Penetration of Internet and broadband into the rural sector, facilitated by government-led initiatives, would make the use of digital technology ubiquitous. This, in turn, would need a demand-driven design and efficient provision of multiple financial products and services through an inclusive financial sector, comprising sustainable institutions serving a diverse rural clientele. Developing and maintaining an inclusive yet sustainable rural financial system would be extremely challenging and would involve comprehensive understanding of a host of inter-connected issues.

More Banks, Better Banking

Recently, the setting up of new banks in the private sector has been driven, among others, by the imperatives of financial inclusion. The transformation of Bandhan, a well-known MFI into a full-fledged commercial bank in 2015, and subsequent issuance of licences to eight MFIs for conversion to Small Finance Banks (SFBs) with focus on financial services to the lower income people have underlined the strategic importance of financial inclusion in shaping the contours of banking in the country. These banks, with their deep insight into rural finance and rich experience at the field level would perhaps make a difference to the manner in which rural banking is conducted in the country. The only problem could be their absence of nation-wide reach and the expectation that they would be lending only to the lower end of the spectrum. They have not only to adhere to the risk management practices for lending to small segments but in the process they have to ensure their own operational viability. The RBI had also announced in August 2016 that on-tap licensing of universal banks would be available on the ground and that such a policy would increase the level of competition and bring new ideas into the system. The new ideas, it is hoped, could also relate to the field of rural banking and financial inclusion.

Similar has been the expectations from the Payments Banks, which would operate on a robust technological platform and offer cost-effective services, although there are many unknown unknowns in respect of these banks. With the banking regulator taking up an innovative approach to the establishment of new differentiated banks and allowing universal banks as and when considered necessary, one can expect several more banks to dot the financial horizon; with competition and more innovations in rural finance with banks also looking at value for their money to remain alive, the field is likely to be much more exciting and challenging.

The establishment of the India Post Payments Bank by the Government of India, several commentators feel, could be a game-changer in the field of financial inclusion in the country. India Post, with its long tradition of postal service, as also payments service, rendered in rural areas, was always a strong candidate for being a bank, except that it had no experience in matters relating to lending, which is a major banking function. It is, therefore, perhaps fine that it has been issued a Payments Bank licence. Its network will come handy in providing deposits and remittance or payments services in the far-flung areas of the country.

Building up Credit Culture

For obvious reasons, banks will continue to be under pressure to achieve lending targets for the priority sector, which in all likelihood, will continue in the foreseeable future. They will have to evolve an appropriate internal system, which must be able to deal with such directed lending, to manage the risks associated with such lending and to vigorously coordinate with government departments and other agencies to ensure proper linkages to borrowers. It will also need a conducive atmosphere in which both suppliers and receivers of financial services can operate without much constraint. To quote Dr Y. V. Reddy, former Governor of the RBI, who first included the term 'financial inclusion' in the RBI's policy statement in 2005, "The full benefit of financial inclusion requires a strong credit culture that inspires confidence among lenders and borrowers.... We should apply our minds to the issues of credit culture in addition to institutional and legal changes and policy initiatives"[3]. The risks rural borrowers face must be comprehensively addressed so as to ensure that not only are they in a position to make their ends meet and make a decent living but they are also able to repay whatever loan they take from banks. If this is to be ensured, obviously the pressure that banks face for fulfilling lending targets must be moderated and banks must be given the freedom to choose borrowers and have a proper appraisal of loan proposals.

Any agricultural loan waiver in future, if at all resorted to, must be based on the objective criterion of crop loss suffered by the farmer rather than waiver across the table in which the honest borrower is generally sidelined and there is no way to distinguish between a person who has been affected by a natural calamity and another who just avoids paying to the bank, expecting a waiver at some point of time. Data on crop yield must be made available by the state government as quickly as possible, certainly within a reasonable timeframe. All decisions as to what support would be needed to be given to farmers should be based on available data, and not on one's whims and fancies. There should not be any issue if those who are actually affected by a calamity have their loans waived. The bank can be compensated from a fund set up for the purpose. Apart from rigorous analytical exercise, however, it would require great political will to implement such a waiver on the basis of the actual loss suffered. With loan waivers becoming part of the electoral promise in several states and the credit culture getting more vitiated with every passing year, the system is fast reaching its tolerance limit and one can only hope for the situation to improve at some point.

Informed Credit Decisions

Assessing the creditworthiness of prospective borrowers has been a major task for bankers. They have developed a time-tested mechanism to identify viable economic activities as also creditworthy borrowers. Of late, credit bureaus and credit information companies have come to their aid by developing algorithm-based credit scores of individuals, which have come handy at the time of loan appraisal. This has to a certain extent addressed the information asymmetry inherent in any interaction between a bank and its borrowers. However, this system has not helped much in the case of millions of rural borrowers, a majority of whom save and borrow small amounts, leave alone the first-time borrowers who have no credit history. Although it is mandatory for banks in India to be a member of at least one credit information company, the database of these companies does not contain detailed credit information in respect of such rural borrowers, especially those availing micro credit through a group mode.

As per the RBI guidelines to banks in June 2014 and subsequently clarified in the light of recommendations of a working group in January 2016, credit as well as some non-credit information in respect of SHG members is required to be furnished to the credit information companies within a timeframe. However, banks have been inconvenienced by the fact that so far they were dealing with only the groups and not their members. That is how the SHG-Bank Linkage Programme had started and had progressed. Now, banks have to maintain data of all individual members of SHGs, which in itself is a herculean task. In view of the importance of such a database, it is expected that in due course, they would comply with the requirement and in that case, information of rural borrowers would be available to banks for examination at the time of appraising a loan proposal, whether from an individual or from a group.

Linking financial services provided by banks with the Aadhaar numbers of the individuals availing the services can also be of help in building a database. In fact, the Committee on Medium Term Path on Financial Inclusion, set up by the RBI, had, in its report submitted in December 2015, recommended that credit history of all SHG members would need to be created, linking it to individual Aadhaar numbers, which would ensure credit discipline and provide comfort to banks.

Aligning with Tomorrow's Technologies

We have seen how technology is shaping financial services delivery and we know that technology will be driving growth in this area in future. There would be more innovative ways of interacting with customers. Continued innovation in products and business models would be needed so that we can reach more people with a broader range of products at lower costs. No one type of provider will be able to overcome the very different business model challenges of all products. What is needed instead is a variety of financial service providers that come together in an ecosystem that works for the poor at the base of the economic pyramid. One such partnership can be between banks and the newly emerging FinTech companies. In the last few years, banks have been increasingly collaborating with such companies to provide convenience and better services to customers in a collaborative and cost-effective way, instead of going on their own. It is this collaborative action that has the potential to alter the financial landscape substantially.

FinTech companies bring in new technologies and innovation that aims to compete with traditional ways of delivering financial services. This is a rapidly evolving segment of the financial services sector where technology-focused start-ups and other new market entrants are disrupting how the financial services industry traditionally operates, with their innovations. At this stage, conditions in India seem to be suitable for development of the FinTech sector with a large market of under-served or un-served customers on one hand and increasing mobile penetration, an active start-up ecosystem and large technology talent pool available in the country on the other hand which can be harnessed for the purpose.

Several experts have opined that in the field of banking, the next wave of innovations in the technology space can relate to digital payments, integrated digital banking, machine learning and artificial intelligence (AI), robo-advisory, augmented and virtual reality, block-chain technology and tackling cyber and financial crime. The digital transformation has been truly astounding, dramatically shifting customer behaviour and their expectations from their financial service providers. It has shown new and innovative ways to spend, move and manage our money. In all these areas and more to come, mainstream banking institutions would continue to collaborate with FinTech companies to deliver innovative customer service and improve upon existing service delivery.

A Working Group on FinTech and Digital Banking, appointed by the RBI, had in its report (November 2017) detailed the various ways in which FinTech can be used to further financial inclusion in the country[4]. These could relate to easy cash transfer, integration of Aadhaar infrastructure, enhanced mobile banking, digitisation of land records, direct account transfer, crop insurance, introduction of UID for MSME borrowers and cyber security, etc., through development of suitable apps or otherwise. With a collaborative, rather than disruptive approach, FinTech companies offer promises to bridge the gaps in efficient financial services delivery, and the financial sector players, including banks, insurance companies and other entities, will increasingly collaborate with these start-ups in future.

With increase in the use of digital technology and the continuous advancement in technology application in financial matters in an increasingly inter-connected world, cyber security is going to be of utmost concern to service providers. We have seen how digital payment systems have been consciously and enthusiastically promoted by the government and banks, and how much energy and resources are spent in spreading digital literacy among people. The efforts are sure to multiply, with special emphasis on meeting cyber threats that would surely be there in more virulent forms as more and more people use the Internet for carrying out financial transactions.

More Collaborations

Rural finance in India has been part of a broader development agenda. The process of social and economic development is essentially a collaborative process. There are several institutions, which at any given point of time take care of different aspects of the development process, and all of them must act in coordination for true progress to happen. The same is true for provision of financial services. The challenges facing rural financial institutions in India are formidable, and no single institution will be able to meet the needs of a diverse and heterogeneous population, a significant part of which is poor. Banks, insurance companies and other financial institutions have been working side by side with development agencies, both in the government and non-government sectors, to see that available funds are properly utilised for development. Effectiveness of their action has been to a great extent a result of such collaborative working. Similarly, financial inclusion has also been a collaborative process, as we have seen before. This will be more emphasised in future, as individual institutions become more and more specialised and would, therefore, need the support of other institutions to ensure holistic and meaningful inclusion. Apart from technology providers, banks would need to intensify collaboration with non-banking financial companies, NGOs, the government, as well as the corporate sector.

While this would ensure provision of financial services at the individual level, there would be a greater need for collaboration at the level of infrastructure creation, particularly for agriculture and related activities, which would ultimately impact provision of finance to these sectors. This would need to be addressed at the sector level and would involve larger capital requirements. At present, the creation of infrastructure in the rural sector involving larger outlay of funds is primarily the responsibility of the government, with the private sector playing a supportive role, especially at a micro level. The existing gap in infrastructure can be bridged through a collaborative public-private partnership approach, through which new institutional arrangements can emerge.

A Note of Caution

In the entire process, however, we need to guard against too much supply side pressure and need to concentrate more and more on the demand side dynamics. Nothing can be more harmful to the system than a sense of helplessness in the target group for which major steps have been taken and are continuing to be taken for making available financial services. The steps taken need to be woven into the ecosystem and they must respond to the person's needs, not only once but on a continuing basis. The person for whom all this is meant must feel comfortable with it and must be confident to use it when the occasion arises. Only then the efforts can be deemed to be successful. We have seen that provision of financial services or the financial inclusion efforts have been more successful in areas which are economically more developed and areas which have the potential for some economic activity to be undertaken, which in turn is a function of infrastructure, education, health and certain related parameters. On the other hand, we have also seen how well intentioned efforts at bringing about financial inclusion in highly underdeveloped areas with practically no infrastructure worth its name, have suffered. The learning point is that people's aspirations must be kept in view while making any attempt at effective financial inclusion and that the demand and supply side initiatives must converge. In future, the role of the government and the financial sector would be to facilitate this convergence.

Notes and References

Chapter 1: Financial Services in Rural India – Work in Progress

1. East Godavari District of Andhra Pradesh was the first to implement the Aadhaar Enabled Payment System (AEPS). It was inaugurated in Gollaprolu village of East Godavari District in January 2013 by the then Union Minister, Jairam Ramesh. With the launch of the scheme, FINO Paytech, a Business Correspondent of ICICI Bank, would facilitate MGNREGA and pension payments through Aadhaar-linked bank accounts to the identified beneficiaries.
2. Changing Structure of Rural Economy of India – Implications for Employment and Growth, by Ramesh Chand, S. K. Srivastava and Jaspal Singh, NITI Aayog, November 2017.
3. As the finance from private sources was not adequate, the state had to step in to provide assistance to farmers in the form of Taccavi loans, mostly for relieving distress but also for developmental purpose. Planning Commission – First Five Year Plan document – chapter on Finance for Agriculture.
4. Result of All India Rural Credit Survey 1950-51. Subsequently, data on indebtedness are obtained through All India Debt and Investment Survey, starting 1960-61 by the RBI, and from 1970-71 onwards by Government of India, National Sample Survey Organisation (NSSO).
5. Financial inclusion started by offering a 'no-frills' bank account, subsequently renamed as 'basic savings bank deposit account (BSBDA)'.
6. Reserve Bank of India – Mid-Term Review of Annual Policy Statement for 2005-06, 25 October, 2005.

Chapter 2: The Supply Push – Challenges of the Last Mile

1. The Indian Cooperative Credit Societies Act, 1904 and 1912.

2-3. Report on Trend and Progress of Banking in India 2016-17 – the Reserve Bank of India.

4. In terms of the Banking Regulation Act (as Applicable to Cooperative Societies), 1966. Cooperative Banks were also brought under the Deposit Insurance Scheme with effect from this date.
5. Report on Trend and Progress of Banking in India 2016-17 – the Reserve Bank of India.

6. The Rural Credit Survey Committee, established by the RBI under the Chairmanship of A. D. Gorwala, ICS (Retd) in 1951, submitted its report in 1954, which inter alia recommended strengthening of the three-tier cooperative credit structure in the country. See 'The Reserve Bank and Rural Credit', published by the RBI, 1985.
7. Report of the Task Force on Revival of the Rural Cooperative Credit Institutions, February 2005. The Task Force made several suggestions including a financial package for cleaning up the balance sheets of the Short Term Cooperative Credit Institutions, along with legal and institutional reforms necessary to make the cooperative banks conform to the basic principles of cooperation.
8. The capital requirement for banks in the private sector is quite stiff. Even in the case of NBFCs, the capital required is Rs 2 crore. Hence, for a cooperative society to become a bank and be able to comply with the prudential requirements, the initial capital must be at a higher level, say, at least Rs 1 crore.
9. Report on Trend and Progress of Banking in India, 2016-17 – the Reserve Bank of India, 21 December 2017.

10-11. Same as above.

12-15. The Reserve Bank of India, various reports and statistics.

16. The Reserve Bank of India circular dated 25 January, 2006 – Financial Inclusion by Extension of Banking Services – Use of Business Facilitators and Business Correspondents.
17. The Reserve Bank of India Annual Report – Various periods.
18. NABARD Annual Report.

19-20. Local Area Banks in India: A Review; M S Sriram, June 2014

21. A Hundred Small Steps – Report of the Committee on Financial Sector Reforms, 2009.
22. The Reserve Bank of India: Revised Regulatory Framework for NBFCs – circular dated November 10, 2014.
23. Mohammed Yunus: Banker to the Poor – The Story of Grameen Bank.

24-25. NABARD: Microfinance in India 2016-17.

26. Microfinance Industry in India; Lok Capital, March 2010.
27. Microsave India Focus Note 40 – State of Microfinance in India 2010; Jaspreet Singh, May 2010.
28. The Andhra Pradesh Microfinance Institutions (Regulation of Moneylending) Ordinance, October 2010. In December 2010 this ordinance was enacted into The Andhra Pradesh Microfinance Institutions (Regulation of Moneylending) Act, 2010.

29. The Microfinance Institutions (Development and Regulation) Bill, which sought to provide a statutory framework for regulation and development of the microfinance industry in India.
30. Study on Costs and Margins of Microfinance Institutions, 2006: Dash R. N. and Murray E. V.; College of Agricultural Banking, Pune. *www.cab.org.in*
31. Cost of Delivering Rural Credit in India: Anand Sahasranaman & Deepti George, IFMR Finance Foundation; April 2013.
32. Re-prioritizing Priority Sector Lending in India – Impact of Priority Sector Lending on India's Commercial Banks; Nathan Associates Inc., Economic Impact Analysis, December 2013.
33. Insurance Regulatory and Development Authority of India; *www.irdai.gov.in*
34. RBI Press Release dated 23 June, 2017 on amendment to the Banking Ombudsman Scheme 2006; *www.rbi.org.in*
35. Data as on 4 April 2018. *www.pmjdy.gov.in*

Chapter 3: The Demand Factor – Facilitating the First Mile Walk

1. Portfolios of the Poor – How the World's Poor Live on $2 a Day: Daryl Collins, Jonathan Morduch, Stuart Rutherford and Orlanda Ruthven; Princeton University Press, 2009.
2. Vijay Mahajan: The Future of Rural Finance in India: Valedictory lecture, National Seminar on Changing Perspective of Rural Finance and Financial Inclusion of Rural Poor; National Institute of Rural Development and Panchayati Raj (NIRD&PR), Hyderabad; April 2017.
3. Financial Inclusion at the Bottom of the Pyramid by Carol Realini and Karl Mehta; Friesen Press, 2015.
4. Financial Literacy Around the World: The Standard and Poors Rating Services Global Financial Literacy Survey, 2014.
5. Who Moved My Interest Rate – Leading the Reserve Bank Through Five Turbulent Years: Subbarao Duvvuri.
6. Section 26A of the Banking Regulation Act empowers the RBI to establish a Depositor Education and Awareness Fund. Money lying in unclaimed deposits with banks in India for a period of 10 years is credited to this Fund, which is used for promotion of depositors' interest and related matters. See the RBI circular dated 21 March, 2014: *www.rbi.org.in*
7. *www.rudsetacademy.org* – National Academy of Rudsetis.
8. The Financial Resolution and Deposit Insurance Bill, 2016 can be seen at *www.dea.gov.in*. Certain provisions of the Bill have been discussed in great detail in most leading newspapers.
9. The Banking Ombudsman Scheme: Annual Report 2016-17 at *www.rbi.org.in*

Chapter 4: Policy Making – Changing Focus, Adapting to Change

1. The All India Debt and Investment Survey, NSSO, Government of India.
2. Report on Trend and Progress of Banking in India, 2016-17: Reserve Bank of India, December 2017.
3. After the setting up of NABARD, Section 54 of the Reserve Bank of India Act, 1934 was amended to allow it to maintain expert staff to study various aspects of rural credit and development and in particular to tender expert guidance and assistance to NABARD, and to conduct special studies in such areas as it may consider necessary to do so for promoting integrated rural development. In fact, the policy statements announced by the RBI contain, among others, specific developmental measures which impact the rural and priority sector credit.
4. RBI Master Circular on Lending to Priority Sector: *www.rbi.org.in*
5. Report of the RBI Internal Group on Priority Sector Lending, March 2015: see on the RBI website.
6. Financial Stability Report – December 2017, the Reserve Bank of India.
7. Rising NPAs in Education Loan adds to banks' stress – Business Today, 24 December 2017. The news appeared in most of the leading newspapers on that date.
8. Affordable Housing in India – the RBI Monthly Bulletin, January 2018. The NPA level of 10.4 per cent is in respect of both PSBs and HFCs. In case of PSBs only, the NPA in loans up to Rs 2 lakh is 11.9 per cent.
9. NSSO Situational Assessment Survey of Farmers, 2013.
10. A study by the National Institute of Rural Development and Panchayati Raj (NIRD&PR) shows that about 39 per cent of respondent farmers had made only one withdrawal and another 46 per cent had made two withdrawals during the last one year.
11. Definition of agriculture as per NABARD Act, 1981, Section 2.
12. Details of the scheme can be found at the website of the Agriculture Insurance Company of India Ltd., *www.aicofindia.com*
13. CAG Report dated 21 July, 2017 on Performance Audit of Union Government Agriculture Crop Insurance Scheme. Among others, the report also highlighted the low coverage of farmers under the schemes, reporting that the share of farmers covered under all crop insurance schemes ranged between 8 to 22 per cent of the total farmers, between Kharif and Rabi crops from 2011 to 2016.
14. From Plate to Plough: Premium Delayed, Farmer Denied – Ashok Gulati & Siraj Hussain; The Indian Express, May 14, 2018

15. Report on Crop Loan Waiver Scheme in Telangana State; Dr B. Yerram Raju, February 2017. The study also cites international experiences in crop insurance, especially in the USA and South Korea and observes that the PMFBY should move away from area-based approach to farmer-based approach, taking advantage of modern technology linked to GIS and remote sensing applications.
16. For example, the Advisory Committee on Flow of Credit to Agriculture and Related Activities from the Banking System (Vyas Committee), 2004 had in its report recommended an Agri-Risk Fund, with equal contribution from the Central and State Governments and the participating banks. Such a fund, the Committee felt, would mitigate the risk of the lending banks as they can have recourse to the fund in the event of genuine default; it would also mitigate the hardship of farmers.
17. NABARD Annual Report 2017-18.
18. The Fourth Census of Micro, Small and Medium Enterprises in India; *www.dcmsme.gov.in*
19. Three companies have been licensed by the RBI for launching TReDS. These are (i) RXIL set up by NSE and SIDBI, (ii) M1 Exchange set up by Mynd Solutions, and (iii) Invoicemart set up by Axis Bank.
20. State of the Agent Network, India 2017 – Microsave Helix Institute of Digital Finance.
21. Planning Commission, Government of India, Paper on IRDP by Dr N. C. Saxena, Former Secretary, Planning Commission.
22. Also see 'Good Governance and Poverty Alleviation Programmes: A Critical Analysis of SGSY' by H. S. Sylendra and Kishore Bhirdikar, IRMA Working Paper 190, July 2005.
23. Independent Assessment of Design, Strategies, and Impacts of DAY-NRLM; Institute of Rural Management Anand, submitted to the Government of India, Ministry of Rural Development.
24. See *www.rsetimis.org*

Chapter 5: Technology – Enabling the Enabler

1. The Reserve Bank of India, Annual Report – 2016-17.
2. The EBT was also adopted in Haryana, Karnataka, Odisha, Chhattisgarh, Himachal Pradesh, Uttarakhand, Bihar and Punjab to varying degrees. The Reserve Bank of India: Operational guidelines on implementation of EBT and its convergence with Financial Inclusion Plans (FIP) – August 2011.
3. The matter was flagged at various meetings. Special meetings were also convened by the SLBC to discuss the issue and find a solution. But no acceptable solution emerged.

4. Data available at the NPCI website: *www.npci.org.in*
5. Reports by the RBI, various dates; see *www.rbi.org.in*

Chapter 6: The Road Ahead

1. For Inclusix 2016, see *www.crisil.com*
2. Vision of the Future – Financial Inclusion 2025; CGAP Publication, June 2017.
3. Advice and Dissent – My Life in Public Service; Y. V. Reddy. Published by Harper Business, 2017.
4. Report of the Working Group on Digital Banking, the Reserve Bank of India, November 2017. The report also referred to the need for increasing levels of awareness/education of customers, which should be highlighted by all market regulators as well as the self-regulatory body for FinTech companies.

Index